CHRISTIAN
ROMAN EMPIRE
SERIES

Vol. 14

ON THE

DEATHS

OF THE

PERSECUTORS

A TRANSLATION OF
DE MORTIBUS PERSECUTORUM

by
Lucius Cæcilius Firmianus
Lactantius

by
Lord Hailes
(David Dalrymple)

Evolution Publishing
Merchantville NJ
2021

This translation of *De Mortibus Persecutorum*
by Lactantius originally appeared in:

The Ante-Nicene Fathers, Volume 7
Fathers of the Third and Fourth Centuries:
Lactantius, Venantius, Asterius, Victorinus,
Dionysius, Apostolic Teaching and
Constitutions, Homily and Liturgies.
Alexander Roberts and James Donaldson, Editors
1905

Printed in the United States of America

ISBN 978-1-935228-20-2

TABLE OF CONTENTS

PREFACE TO THE 2021 EDITION

You hold in your hands a work of great antiquity and historical import, without which our knowledge of Diocletian's Tetrarchy, the Great Persecution, and the early reign of Constantine would be considerably impoverished. Amazingly, this work was considered lost for hundreds of years until it was rediscovered in the 17th century, preserved in a convent library in Moissac, France. At that time, the manuscript was declared to be the only surviving copy of *De Persecutione* (referred to in this edition as *On the Deaths of the Persecutors*), a work mentioned in an ancient list of the writings of Lactantius compiled by Saint Jerome.[1] This was an incredible discovery that shed immediate light on the reigns of Diocletian and Constantine, providing heretofore unrecorded details of that period of transition from traditional pagan Rome to the Christian Roman Empire.

For decades after its discovery, the authenticity of *On the Deaths of the Persecutors* was a matter of dispute. This debate was settled decisively by French scholar René Pinchon in 1902 who argued successfully in favor of Lactantian authorship. Since then, nearly all scholars have adopted this view.[2]

There are several English translations of *On the Deaths of the Persecutors* available. Those which are more recent tend to be difficult to obtain and far too expensive for the interested general reader. Those versions of the translation which are more easily accessible to students and general readers are almost all badly produced cut-and-paste reprints which often lack any sort of coherent introductory material, notes, references or index. We have aimed for a middle ground with this edition, producing an accessible reprint edition of the translation by Lord Hailes (David Dalrymple) which was completed in 1782[3] and subsequently repurposed for the *Ante-Nicene Fathers* series in 1871 and again in 1905.[4] We have attempted to add sufficient introductory material and commentary but not to the point where it is oppressive. We have also included an updated list of references and further reading as well as an index.

If, upon reading this work, you wish to track down the complete Latin text along with more exhaustive commentary and notes, please consult *De Mortibus Persecutorum* as executed by J. L. Creed in 1984, and published by Clarendon Press. Also noteworthy is the 1965 translation done by Sister Mary Francis MacDonald and published by the Catholic University of America Press as part of the collected volume entitled, *Lactantius: The Minor Works*.

—*Anthony P. Schiavo, Jr.*
Merchantville, NJ
July 2020

NOTES

1. For a detailed discussion of the provenance of *On the Deaths of the Persecutors,* see *De Mortibus Persecutorum* as translated by J. L. Creed, page xlv.
2. The authorship question is covered in great detail in the introduction to Creed's translation, pages xxix–xxxiii, as well as Sr. McDonald's 1965 translation which appears in *The Minor Works* of Lactantius, pages 123–127.
3. For a complete listing of Lord Hailes's works, see: *Dictionary of National Biography, 1885–1900,* Vol. 13 (1888), page 403.
4. See the entry under Roberts and Donaldson in the "Select Bibliography and Further Reading" section for the full reference.

SELECT BIBLIOGRAPHY AND FURTHER READING

Anastos, Milton V. 1967. "The Edict of Milan (313): A Defense of its Traditional Authorship and Designation," *Revue de Études Byzantines*, Vol. 25, pp. 13–41.

Anonymous. Andrew Eastbourne (transl.) 2013. *On the Passion and Translation of Saint Saturninus, Bishop of the City of Toulouse and Martyr.* Accessed November 16, 2020. http://www.tertullian.org/fathers/passion_of_st_saturninus_02_text.htm

Anonymous Valesianus. J. C. Rolfe (transl.) 1939. *Ammianus Marcellinus: History, Volume III: Books 27–31. Excerpta Valesiana.* Harvard University Press, Cambridge, MA.

Aurelius Victor. H. W. Bird (transl.) 1994. *De Cæsaribus*. Liverpool University Press: Liverpool, UK.

Barnes, T. D. 1981. *Constantine and Eusebius.* Oxford University Press: Oxford, UK.

Barnes, T. D. 1976. "Imperial Campaigns, AD 285–311." *Phoenix*, Vol. 30, No. 2, pp. 174–193.

Barnes, T. D. 1973. "Lactantius and Constantine." *The Journal of Roman Studies,* Vol. 63, pp. 29–46.

Barnes, T. D. 2010. "Maxentius and Diocletian," *Classical Philology*, Vol. 105, No. 3, pp. 318–322

Barnes, T. D. 1973. "More Missing Names, AD 260–395." *Phoenix*, Vol. 27, No. 2, pp. 135–155.

Baynes, N. H. 1924. "Two Notes on the Great Persecution." *The Classical Quarterly,* Vol. 18, No. 3/4, pp. 189–194.

Cassius Dio. Earnest Cary (transl.) 1925. *Roman History. Volume VIII.* G. P. Putnam's Sons: New York.

Christensen, A. S. 1980. *Lactantius the Historian: An Analysis of* De Mortibus Persecutorum. Museum Tusculanum Press: Copenhagen.

Christensen, T. Karsten Engelberg (transl.) 2012 [1974] *C. Galerius Valerius Maximinus: Studies in the Politics and Religion of the Roman Empire AD 305–313.* Theological Faculty, Copenhagen University: Copenhagen, Denmark. Accessed November 25, 2020. http://www.patristik.dk/ebog/Maximinus.pdf

Clark, Patrick E. 2017. *Taxation and the Formation of the Late Roman Social Contract*. University of California, Berkeley, PhD dissertation. Accessed September 28, 2020. https://digitalassets.lib.berkeley.edu/etd/ucb/text/Clark_berkeley_0028E_16921.pdf

Cyprian. Phillip Campbell (ed.) 2013. *The Complete Works of Saint Cyprian of Carthage.* Evolution Publishing: Merchantville, NJ.

Digeser, Elizabeth DePalma. 2000. *The Making of a Christian Empire: Lactantius and Rome.* Cornell University Press: Ithaca, NY.

Digeser, Elizabeth DePalma. 1994. "Lactantius and Constantine's Letter to Arles: Dating the *Divine Institutes.*" *Journal of Early Christian Studies*, Vol. 2, No. 1, pp. 33–52. *Project MUSE*, doi:10.1353/earl.0.0205.

Drake, H. A. 1985. "Suggestions of Date in Constantine's Oration to the Saints." *American Journal of Philology,* Vol. 106, No. 3, pp. 335–349.

Edwards, Marc. 1999. "The Constantinian Circle and the Oration to the Saints." *Apologetics in the Christian Empire: Pagans, Jews, and Christians.* Oxford University Press, Oxford, UK.

Eusebius Pamphilus. Anonymous (transl.) 2009 [1845]. *Life of the Blessed Emperor Constantine.* Evolution Publishing: Merchantville, NJ.

Eusebius Pamphilus. Arthur C. McGiffert (transl.) 1890. See entry under Schaff and Wace below.

Eutropius. H. W. Bird. 1993. *Breviarium.* Liverpool University Press: Liverpool, UK.

Filocalus, Furius Dionysius. *The Chronography of AD 354.* Tertullian.org. Accessed September 9, 2020. http://www.tertullian.org/fathers/chronography_of_354_16_chronicle_of_the_city_of_rome.htm

Graser, E. R. 1940. "A text and translation of the Edict of Diocletian," T. Frank (ed.), *An Economic Survey of Ancient Rome Volume V: Rome and Italy of the Empire*, Johns Hopkins Press: Baltimore, MD.

Healy, Patrick J. 1905. *The Valerian Persecution: A Study of the Relations between the Church and State in the Third Century AD.* Houghton, Mifflin & Company: Boston, MA.

Healy, P. (1909). Flavia Domitilla. In *The Catholic Encyclopedia.* Robert Appleton Company: New York. Accessed August 5, 2020 from New Advent: http://www.newadvent.org/cathen/06098b.htm

Jerome. Philip Schaff and Henry Wace, editors. 1893. *Nicene and Post-Nicene Fathers: Second Series, Volume 6: Jerome: Letters and Selected Works.* Christian Literature Publishing Co.: Buffalo, NY.

Jordanes. Charles C. Mierow (transl.) 2006. *The Gothic History of Jordanes.* Evolution Publishing: Merchantville, NJ.

Kyle, D. G. 1998. *Spectacles of Death in Ancient Rome.* Routledge: London.

Lactantius. McDonald, M. F. (transl.) 1964. *The Divine Institutes, I–VII.* Catholic University of America Press: Washington, DC.

Lactantius. J. L. Creed (transl.) 1984. *De Mortibus Persecutorum.* Clarendon Press: Oxford, UK.

Lactantius. McDonald, Mary Francis (transl.). 1965. *Lactantius: The Minor Works.* Catholic University of America Press: Washington, DC.

Livius, Titus. D. Spillan (transl.) 1871. *The History of Rome*. Harper and Sons: New York.

Nixon, C. E. V. and Barbara Saylor Rodgers. 1994. *In Praise of the Later Roman Emperors: The Panegyrici Latini.* University of California Press: Berkeley, CA.

Odahl, Charles. 2004. *Constantine and the Christian Empire.* Routledge: Abingdon, UK.

Pharr, Clyde. 2001. *The Theodosian Code and Novels and the Sirmondian Constitutions.* The Lawbook Exchange: Union City, NJ.

Photius. J. H. Freese (transl.) 1920. *The Library of Photius, Volume I.* The MacMillan Company: New York.

Pliny the Younger. Wynne Williams (transl.) 1990. *Pliny: Correspondence with Trajan from Bithynia, Epistles X 15–121.* Oxford University Press: Oxford, UK.

Roberts, Alexander and James Donaldson, editors. 1905. *The Ante-Nicene Fathers, Volume 7: Fathers of the Third and Fourth Centuries: Lactantius, Venantius, Asterius, Victorinus, Dionysius, Apostolic Teaching and Constitutions, Homily and Liturgies.* Charles Scribner's Sons: New York.

Schaff, Philip and Henry Wace, editors. 1890. *Nicene and Post-Nicene Fathers: Second Series, Volume 1: Eusebius: Church History, Life of Constantine the Great, and Oration in Praise of Constantine.* Christian Literature Publishing Co.: Buffalo, NY.

Schaff, Philip and Henry Wace, editors. 1892. *Nicene and Post-Nicene Fathers, Second Series, Volume 3: Theodoret, Jerome, Gennadius, Rufinus: Historical Writings, etc.*, Christian Literature Publishing Co.: Buffalo, NY.

Smith, William (editor) 1880. *A Dictionary of Greek and Roman Biography and Mythology.* John Murray: London.

Southern, P. 2015. *The Roman Empire from Severus to Constantine.* Routledge: London.

Sozomen. E. Walford (transl.) 2018 [1885]. *The Ecclesiastical History of Sozomen: From AD 324 to AD 425.* Evolution Publishing: Merchantville, NJ

Suetonius. J. C. Rolfe (transl.) 1914. *Suetonius II.* Harvard University Press: Cambridge, MA.

Sulpicius Severus. Alexander Roberts (transl.) 1894. *Nicene and Post-Nicene Fathers, Second Series, Volume 11: Sulpicius Severus, Vincent of Lerins and John Cassian.* Christian Literature Publishing Co.: Buffalo, NY.

Tacitus. John Jackson (transl.) 1937. *Annals.* Harvard University Press: Cambridge, MA.

Tertullian. T. Herbert Bindley (transl.) 1914. *On the Testimony of the Soul and On the "Prescription" of Heretics.* Society for Promoting Christian Literature Company, New York.

Williams, Stephen. 1996. *Diocletian and the Roman Recovery.* Routledge: New York.

Zosimus. 1814. *New History.* Green and Chaplin: London.

INTRODUCTION[1]

Though an early Latin Church father of great repute and an associate of Constantine the Great, the origins of Lactantius remain obscure. Indeed, even his name is the subject of some confusion though he is often known by his full Roman name: Lucius Cæcilius Firmianus Lactantius. Saint Jerome, in his work *On Illustrious Men*, provides much of what we know for certain about the life of Lactantius:

> Firmianus, known also as Lactantius, a disciple of Arnobius, during the reign of Diocletian summoned to Nicomedia with Flavius the Grammarian whose poem *On Medicine* is still extant, taught rhetoric there and on account of his lack of pupils (since it was a Greek city) he betook himself to writing. We have a *Banquet* of his which he wrote as a young man in Africa and an *Itinerary* of a journey from Africa to Nicomedia written in hexameters, and another book which is called *The Grammarian* and a most beautiful one *On the Wrath of God,* and *Divine Institutes* against the nations, seven books, and an *Epitome* of the same work in one volume, without a title, also two books *To Asclepiades*, one book *On Persecution*, four books of *Epistles* to Probus, two books of *Epistles* to Severus, two books of *Epistles* to his pupil Demetrius and one book to the same *On the Work of God or the Creation of Man*.[2]

In his old age he was tutor to Crispus Cæsar, a son of Constantine, in Gaul—the same one who was afterwards put to death by his father.

Since Lactantius is spoken of as being elderly by AD 315, he was most likely born about the middle of the 3rd century, probably in Africa, though Italy was preferred by earlier scholars. He therefore likely grew up during the Christian persecutions of Decius and Valerian of the 250s though he himself was a pagan at that time. He certainly studied in Africa where he became the pupil of Arnobius,[3] who taught rhetoric at Sicca. His fame as a rhetoritician eventually surpassed that of his master, and by about AD 300, he was invited by Diocletian to settle at Nicomedia, and there to practice his art. The teacher of Latin eloquence, however, found so little encouragement in a city whose population was chiefly Greek, that he was reduced to poverty. He subsequently abandoned his profession and devoted himself entirely to literary composition.

While Lactantius was in Nicomedia, the Great Persecution of Christians under Diocletian and Galerius broke out. It is possible that Lactantius's period of indigence corresponds with his conversion to Christianity, and that his change of religion may even have been the cause of his poverty, for it is unlikely that he would have been left without support by the emperor had he not in some way forfeited the patronage of the imperial court. His position as a well-educated man in the capital of the eastern Augustus gave Lactantius a ring-side seat for the great debates of the philosophical elite as they hashed out a strategy to solve the Christian problem in the early 4th century AD. It was here that he heard the arguments against Christianity made by men like Sossianus Hierocles, governor of Bithynia, and the Neoplatonist philosopher, Porphyry of Tyre.[4] And it was here that he formulated his epic response to them which would later be published as *The Divine Institutes*. It is very likely that during his stay in Nicomedia, Lactantius first became acquainted with a young officer of Diocletian's court—

Constantine, son of the Western Cæsar, Constantius.

We know nothing more of Lactantius's career until we find him summoned to Gaul to oversee the education of Crispus, son of Constantine. This happened near the end of Lactantius's life as indicated by Jerome above, probably at some point during the years AD 310–318. During this time, it is likely that Lactantius played a role in instructing the emperor himself as well. Indeed, one can hear clear echoes of Lactantius's own writings in Constantine's *Oration to the Saints* and later edicts. At least one modern scholar posits that Lactantius embarked on a program of instruction within the court of Constantine at Trier, using *The Divine Institutes* as a guide.[5]

It is believed that Lactantius died at Trier some ten or twelve years afterwards, probably about AD 325.

WORKS[6]

The most well-known and influential work of Lactantius is *The Divine Institutes*, or *Introduction to True Religion*, in seven books, designed to supplement the less complete treatises of Minucius Felix, Tertullian, and Cyprian. In these books, each of which has a distinct title and constitutes a separate essay, Lactantius attempts to demonstrate the falsehood of pagan polytheistic religious beliefs, to show the vanity of the heathen philosophy, and to defend the Christian religion against its adversaries, particularly the Neoplatonist philosophers he had encountered in Nicomedia. He also sets forth the nature of righteousness, gives instructions concerning the true worship of God, and treats of the punishment of the wicked and the reward of the righteous in everlasting happiness.

To the *Divine Institutes* is appended an epitome dedicated to Pentadius. The authorship of this abridgment has been questioned in modern times, but it is expressly assigned to Lactantius by Saint Jerome.

The treatise entitled *On the Anger of God* is directed mainly against the tenets of the Epicureans and Stoics, who maintained that the deeds of men could produce no emotions of pleasure or anger in the Deity. In this treatise, Lactantius holds that the love of the good necessarily implies the hatred of evil, and that the tenets of these philosophers, as tending to overthrow the doctrine of future rewards and punishments, are subversive of the principles of true religion.

In the treatise *On the Workmanship of God*, or *The Formation of Man*, Lactantius dwells upon the wonderful construction of the human frame, and the adaptation of means to ends displayed therein, as proofs of the wisdom and goodness of God. The latter part of the book contains speculations concerning the nature and origin of the soul.

Also extant is a fragment of a work attributed to Lactantius entitled *On the Motions of the Soul*, which was discovered in an 8th or 9th century Milanese manuscript.[7]

Two poetical works occasionally attributed to Lactantius, *The Phœnix* and *On the Passion of the Lord*, are of dubious authenticity. Neither is considered a true work of Lactantius by most scholars.

Several works of the Lactantian corpus as mentioned by St. Jerome above are considered lost. Among these, there is *The Symposium*, often confused with a different work entitled *A Hundred Enigmas* which was dedicated to someone named Symposius. Also lost are the works entitled *Itinerary* and *The Grammarian*. None of the epistolary books of Lactantius seem to have survived aside from a few brief fragments.

It is Lactantius's treatise entitled *On the Deaths of the Persecutors* which concerns us here in this text. In this unique work, Lactantius creates a hybrid of history and apologetics, making an argument for the truth of the Christian religion based on the fates of those emperors who had been the most egregious persecutors of Christians. As a work of history, *On the Deaths of the Persecutors* is a key source for Diocletian's Tetrarchy, the Great Persecution, and the rise of Constantine, worthy to supplement the monumental *Ecclesiastical History* and *The Life of the Blessed Emperor Constantine*, both by Eusebius Pamphilus, as the most important primary sources for this era of transition, turmoil and consolidation.

ON THE DEATHS OF THE PERSECUTORS AS HISTORY

On the Deaths of the Persecutors is a work of considerable historical import containing details about the Roman Empire of the early 4th century AD that are found nowhere else. As much of Lactantius's literary output is apologetic in nature, it is not surprising that his singular work of history also serves such a function. Indeed, the purpose of the work, as Lactantius himself explains in the first chapter, is to demonstrate via a study of history, how God has seen fit to destroy those who are opposed to His will. Regarding the persecuting emperors, he says:

> "Of the end of those men I have thought good to publish a narrative, that all who are afar off, and all who shall arise hereafter, may learn how the Almighty manifested His power and sovereign greatness in rooting out and utterly destroying the enemies of His name."[8]

The style of Lactantius has often been praised. As a Latin rhetor, he valued beauty of language, and his inclusion of Virgilian allusions and quotations to give emphasis to certain parts of his narrative has been remarked

by many scholars. In a letter to St. Paulinus of Nola,
St. Jerome praises Lactantius's style while at the same time
criticizing him for his faults as an apologist: "Lactantius
has a flow of eloquence worthy of Tully [that is, Cicero]:
would that he had been as ready to teach our doctrines as
he was to pull down those of others!"[9] In the present work,
Lactantius utilizes his literary gifts to give a vivid insider's
account of how the persecuting emperors ruled, drawing a
straight line between their brutal acts against the empire's
Christian minority, and the pathetic or horrifying ends they
later endured.

To introduce his theme, Lactantius briefly describes
the fates of the Roman imperial persecutors of Christians
prior to the time of his writing, namely Nero, Domitian,
Decius, Valerian and Aurelian. In these chapters, which
are little more than summaries, hardly any new or unique
information is conveyed. Once Lactantius shifts to his
own time period, however, the value of his historical
testimony rises dramatically. Of course, one should
bear in mind while reading this work that Lactantius is
nothing like a dispassionate observer of historical events
and actions. Furthermore, his account does not follow a
strict chronological order. He sees his work as a teachable
moment—an opportunity to instruct his audience on the
truths of the Christian religion, while at the same time
reminding them of the malign and often horrific destinies of
those who saw fit to destroy the Church and make martyrs
of the saints.

On the Deaths of the Persecutors focuses on the reigns
of the four original co-emperors who ruled under a scheme
commonly called the Tetrarchy, a novelty which was
imposed upon the Roman state by Diocletian in the late
3rd century AD. Under this system, Diocletian ruled the
East from Nicomedia as Augustus or senior emperor, with

Galerius serving as his Cæsar or junior emperor. In the West, Maximian was appointed Augustus and ruled primarily from Milan, with Constantius Chlorus as his Cæsar. Later, Diocletian and Maximian would jointly retire, promoting Galerius and Constantius to the roles of senior Augusti, while two other men, Maximin Daia and Severus, were raised to the rank of Cæsars. The complexities, jealousies, and conflicts associated with these transactions are recorded nowhere better than by Lactantius in the present work.

Diocletian's accession ended a thirty year period of political and military turmoil within the Roman Empire which nearly led to complete dissolution on several occasions—the so-called Crisis of the 3rd Century. After consolidating his power in the late 280s, Diocletian engaged in a wide-ranging program of reform in an attempt to strengthen and reorganize the empire from within. While modern scholars have tended to look favorably on these reforms, they have had to do so while discounting the harsh critiques of Diocletian's policies which are everywhere present in *On the Deaths of the Persecutors*.

Of course, the persecution of Christians under the Tetrarchy may be viewed as part of this systematic reform. Like Decius and Valerian before them, Diocletian and Galerius came to view the Christians as an internal fifth column—an organized, disloyal institution operating in the shadows but with increasing boldness. Worse, because they refused to worship the cult of the Roman state, Christians were viewed as angering the very gods who protected the empire and defended the emperors. It was believed by many that Roman peace and tranquility could only be maintained if the traditional Roman pantheon was worshipped correctly.[10] Spurred on by court philosophers as mentioned above, and especially by the insistent cajolery of his colleague, Galerius, Diocletian would embark upon the most violent, systematic, wide-ranging, and brutal persecution of Christians that the Roman Empire had ever attempted.

Lactantius was an eye-witness to these events. Though his vantage point is not always clear, we do know that he spent considerable time in Diocletian's capital, Nicomedia, which was the center of much of the action. For the behind-the-scenes details on the run-up to the persecution, the early life of Constantine as a hostage at the court of Diocletian, the events leading up to the resignation of Diocletian and Maximian in AD 305, and the subsequent surprise accessions of Maximin Daia and Severus, there is no better extant source than *On the Deaths of the Persecutors*. As the Great Persecution was launched from Nicomedia, Lactantius provides a descriptive and tantalizing account of the initial stages, including the suspicious fires at the imperial palace, the events surrounding the issuance of the edict of persecution, and the demolition of the great church of Nicomedia, a large edifice which was apparently visible from the palace.

To a certain extent, *On the Deaths of the Persecutors* climaxes with Lactantius's horrifying account of the death of the prime motivator of the Great Persecution, Galerius, who ruled the East as Augustus following the resignation of Diocletian. Lactantius covers the gruesome sickness and death of Galerius in macabre detail, reminiscent of the death of Antiochus IV as recorded in 2 Maccabees 9 and Herod Agrippa in Acts 12:23. As Galerius approaches his excruciating denouement, he extends his stunning edict of toleration to the Christians (which Lactantius quotes in full) offering feeble excuses for his previous brutality and asking the followers of Christ to pray for him, for the state, and for themselves.[11] This edict of toleration, revoked by Maximin Daia soon after, presaged that of Constantine and Licinius—

the famous Edict of Milan—which was issued in AD 313.

Lactantius seems to have been a witness to events in the West beginning at some point after AD 310 when he joined the court of Constantine. Constantine had escaped to Britain and following the death of his father, Constantius, he was acclaimed emperor at York in AD 306. Some time afterwards, Lactantius was appointed tutor to Constantine's son, Crispus. Though he likely arrived too late to witness events first-hand, Lactantius was no doubt able to collect accounts from the followers of Constantine and possibly from the emperor himself. His reports on the treachery and execution of Maximian, the final insanity and death of Diocletian, and the civil war between Constantine and Maxentius are all extremely valuable, though bearing the obvious stamp of Constantinian propaganda.

Also among these passages, we find Lactantius's account of the dream of Constantine, wherein that emperor was advised to have his soldiers paint the Christian chi-rho symbol on their shields. It is interesting to compare this passage with the more detailed account of Eusebius Pamphilus in his *Life of the Blessed Emperor Constantine*, which says, quoting Constantine himself:

> "He said that about mid-day, when the sun was beginning to decline, he saw with his own eyes the trophy of a cross of light in the heavens, above the sun, and bearing the inscription, 'Conquer by this.' At this sight, he himself was struck with amazement, and his whole army also....He said, moreover, that he doubted within himself what the import of this apparition could be. And while he continued to ponder and reason on its meaning, night imperceptibly drew on, and in his sleep the Christ of God appeared to him with the same sign

which he had seen in the heavens, and commanded him to procure a standard made in the likeness of that sign, and to use it as a safeguard in all engagements with his enemies."[12]

Though these accounts align well on the point of the dream, the reader is left to wonder why Constantine decided to confide the additional details only to Eusebius, or why, if Lactantius knew such details, he decided to omit them. What Lactantius offers here is confirmation that Constantine experienced some form of theophany prior to his final encounter with Maxentius and that it was apparently well known at the time.

Lactantius's subsequent coverage of the war between Constantine and Maxentius is cursory and a more detailed account may be found in Eusebius's *Life of Constantine* and in other contemporary accounts. Following the disposal of Maxentius, Lactantius records the conference of Constantine and Licinius at Milan, and later provides the full text of the so-called Edict of Milan which resulted from that meeting.[13]

Lactantius offers a more positive view of Licinius in his narrative than one might expect. Unlike Eusebius who would later paint Licinius with the same brush as the other persecuting emperors, Lactantius takes a more diplomatic approach. This is, no doubt, because Lactantius wrote *On the Deaths of the Persecutors* during the time of truce between Constantine and Licinius, when the latter may have been considered on par with the former by the Christian community for his role in ending the Great Persecution. Yet hints of a change in the winds may be detected even here. For example, in Chapter L, Lactantius mentions how Licinius put to death any who, by familial connection to the persecuting emperors, might have constituted a threat to his rule. Those mentioned included Valeria, daughter of Diocletian and wife of Galerius; Candidianus, the illegitimate son of Galerius; Severianus, son of the short-lived emperor, Severus; the son and daughter of Maximin Daia who were but eight and seven years of age, respectively; and finally, Diocletian's wife who was beheaded along with Valeria. Lactantius gives her name as Prisca and is the only ancient source which provides this information. Lactantius also hints that Prisca, along with her daughter Valeria, may have been among the secret Christians who were part of Diocletian's court when the Great Persecution first erupted, saying that they were the first "to be polluted by sacrificing."[14]

With the final extirpation of the persecuting emperors and the miserable deaths of their family members, Lactantius closes his history. In his last chapter, Lactantius explains how he obtained his information and his ultimate reason for writing:

> "I relate all those things on the authority of well-informed persons, and I thought it proper to commit them to writing exactly as they happened, lest the memory of events so important should perish, and lest any future historian of the persecutors should corrupt the truth."[15]

So without further attempts at explication on the part of the present editor which might corrupt the truth, I invite the reader to dive into this fascinating historical narrative composed by a very well-informed man, perfectly placed to tell the story in lively if occasionally lurid language.

NOTES

1. This introduction is drawn in part from the biography of Lactantius which appears in *A Dictionary of Greek and Roman Biography and*

Mythology (1880), page 701, though it has been heavily edited and re-written for use in the present text.

2. This text was taken from the translation of St. Jerome's *On Illustrious Men* that appeared in *Nicene and Post-Nicene Fathers, Second Series*, Volume 3 by Schaff and Wace (1893).

3. Jerome identifies Arnobius in *On Illustrious Men* as follows: "Arnobius was a most successful teacher of rhetoric at Sicca in Africa during the reign of Diocletian and wrote volumes *Against the Nations* which may be found everywhere."

4. For a very detailed look at these debates, see Digeser, *The Making of a Christian Empire: Lactantius and Rome*, page 3–17.

5. See Digeser, "Lactantius and Constantine's Letter to Arles: Dating the Divine Institutes" in *Journal of Early Christian Studies*, Vol. 2:1, page 51.

6. The "Works" section of this introduction is borrowed from *The Ante-Nicene Fathers, Volume 7: Fathers of the Third and Fourth Centuries* by Roberts and Donaldson (1905), page 5. This text has also been edited and re-written for use in the present volume.

7. A translation of this fragment may be found in McDonald, *Lactantius: The Minor Works*, page 223.

8. *On the Deaths of the Persecutors*, Chapter I.

9. Taken from Letter 58 to Paulinus of Nola which may be found in *The Principle Works of Saint Jerome* from the *Select Library of Nicene and Post-Nicene Fathers*, Second Series, Volume 6, by Schaff and Wace (1892), page 122.

10. See Digeser, *The Making of a Christian Empire: Lactantius and Rome*, page 2–3.

11. See *On the Deaths of the Persecutors*, Chapter XXXIV.

12. Taken from: Eusebius, *Life of the Blessed Emperor Constantine*, Book I, Chapter XXVIII–XXIX.

13. See *On the Deaths of the Persecutors*, Chapter XLVIII.

14. See *On the Deaths of the Persecutors*, Chapter XV.

15. See *On the Deaths of the Persecutors*, Chapter LI.

ON THE DEATHS OF THE
PERSECUTORS

ON THE DEATHS
OF THE PERSECUTORS[1]

ADDRESSED TO DONATUS

CHAPTER I

The Lord has heard those supplications which you, my
best beloved Donatus,[2] pour forth in His presence all the
day long, and the supplications of the rest of our brethren
who by a glorious confession have obtained an everlasting
crown, the reward of their faith. Behold, all the adversaries
are destroyed, and tranquillity having been re-established
throughout the Roman Empire, the late oppressed Church
arises again, and the temple of God, overthrown by the
hands of the wicked, is built with more glory than before.
For God has raised up princes[3] to rescind the impious and
sanguinary edicts of the tyrants and provide for the welfare
of mankind, so that now the cloud of past times is dispelled,
and peace and serenity gladden all hearts. And after the
furious whirlwind and black tempest, the heavens are now
become calm and the wished-for light has shone forth. And
now God, the hearer of prayer, by His divine aid has lifted
His prostrate and afflicted servants from the ground, has
brought to an end the united devices of the wicked, and
wiped off the tears from the faces of those who mourned.

They who insulted over the Divinity lie low. They who
cast down the holy temple are fallen with more tremendous
ruin. And the tormentors of just men have poured out their
guilty souls amidst plagues inflicted by Heaven and amidst

1

deserved tortures. For God delayed to punish them, that by great and marvellous examples, He might teach posterity that He alone is God and that with fit vengeance He executes judgment on the proud, the impious, and the persecutors.[4]

Of the end of those men I have thought good to publish a narrative, that all who are afar off and all who shall arise hereafter may learn how the Almighty manifested His power and sovereign greatness in rooting out and utterly destroying the enemies of His name. And this will become evident when I relate who were the persecutors of the Church from the time of its first constitution, and what were the punishments by which the divine Judge, in His severity, took vengeance on them.

NOTES

1. Of course, the narrative of Lactantius does not include all of the persecutors, but only some of them. The historical character of this document is recognized even by Gibbon who was often harshly critical of Christian sources. See *History of the Decline and Fall of the Roman Empire,* Volume II, Chapter 20.
2. For more about Donatus, to whom Lactantius dedicates this work, see Chapter XVI below. Lactantius also describes the release of Donatus from prison in Chapter XXXV.
3. By princes, Lactantius is referring here to Constantine and Licinius.
4. To this day, one who visits Rome may stand before the Arch of Constantine and, at the same time, behold the Colosseum close at hand. No two symbols of Roman civilization better exemplify this passage whereby pagan Rome gave way to Christian Rome within the lifetime of Lactantius.

CHAPTER II

In the latter days of the Emperor Tiberius, in the consulship of Ruberius Geminus and Fufius Geminus, and on the tenth of the kalends of April,[1] as I find it written, Jesus Christ was crucified by the Jews. After He had risen again on the third day, He gathered together His apostles, whom fear, at the time of His arrest had put to flight. And while He sojourned with them forty days, He opened their hearts, interpreted to them the Scripture which hitherto had been wrapped up in obscurity, ordained and fitted them for the preaching of His word and doctrine, and regulated all things concerning the institutions of the New Testament. And this having been accomplished, a cloud and whirlwind enveloped Him and caught Him up from the sight of men into Heaven.

His apostles were at that time eleven in number, to whom were added Matthias in the room of the traitor Judas, and afterwards Paul. Then were they dispersed throughout all the earth to preach the Gospel as the Lord their Master had commanded them. And during twenty-five years and until the beginning of the reign of the Emperor Nero, they occupied themselves in laying the foundations of the Church in every province and city. And while Nero reigned, the Apostle Peter came to Rome, and through the power of God committed unto him wrought certain miracles, and by turning many to the true religion, built up a faithful and steadfast temple unto the Lord.

When Nero heard of those things and observed that not only in Rome but in every other place a great multitude revolted daily from the worship of idols and condemning their old ways went over to the new religion, he being an execrable and pernicious tyrant, sprung forward to raze the heavenly temple and destroy the true faith. He it was who first persecuted the servants of God. He crucified Peter and slew Paul.[2] Nor did he escape with impunity, for God looked on the affliction of His people, and therefore the tyrant, bereaved of authority and precipitated from the height of empire, suddenly disappeared and even the burial-place of that noxious wild beast was nowhere to be seen. This has led some persons of extravagant imagination to suppose that having been conveyed to a distant region, he is still reserved alive, and to him they apply the Sibylline verses concerning,

"The fugitive, who slew his own mother, being to come from the uttermost boundaries of the earth,"

as if he who was the first should also be the last persecutor, and thus prove the forerunner of Antichrist. But we ought not to believe those who, affirming that the two prophets Enoch and Elias have been translated into some remote place that they might attend our Lord when He shall come to judgment, also fancy that Nero is to appear hereafter as the forerunner of the devil, when he shall come to lay waste the earth and overthrow mankind.[3]

NOTES

1. That is, March 23. Other ancient authorities prefer the date of March 25 for the crucifixion. This date has been a matter of intense scholarly debate across the centuries. For a modern summary of the argument, see Depuydt, "The Date of the Death of Jesus," in *Journal of the American Oriental Society*, Vol. 122, No. 3, pages 466–480. It is not known where Lactantius found this date written.

    The consulship of Ruberius Geminus and Fufius Geminus is mentioned by Tacitus as the year that Julia Augusta perished of old age. Also known as Livia Drusilla, she was the matriarch of the Julio-Claudian imperial family—wife of Augustus Cæsar, mother of Tiberius, and grandmother of Gaius Caligula and Claudius. See *Annals,* Book V, Chapter 1.

2. St. Peter, as a Jew, was liable to crucifixion. St. Paul, as a Roman citizen, was subject to the comparatively more merciful punishment of beheading. Very early accounts of the fates of these Apostles are recorded in *The Ecclesiastical History of Eusebius* (quoting Origen), Book III, Chapter I as well as Tertullian: *On the Testimony of the Soul and On the Prescription of Heretics.* The most well known contemporary account of Nero's persecution from the classical period is the notice in the *Annals* of Tacitus, Book XV, Chapter 44.

3. Nero reigned from AD 54 to AD 68 when he was toppled by Galba. The account of Nero's death here seems to run contrary to the account of Suetonius in *The Lives of the Cæsars*, which records

the details of Nero's suicide. Suetonius claims that his burial place was well known and that, "there were some who for a long time decorated his tomb with spring and summer flowers." Suetonius also mentions that there were rumors that Nero was still alive and would shortly return to visit retribution upon his enemies. See Suetonius, *The Life of Nero*, Chapter 57.

Interestingly, Sulpicius Severus in his *Sacred History* (Book II, Chapter 29), written some 80 to 100 years after Lactantius, seems to corroborate what must have been the commonplace Christian view of Nero's fate, saying: "Nero, now hateful even to himself from a consciousness of his crimes, disappears from among men, leaving it uncertain whether or not he had laid violent hands upon himself: certainly his body was never found. It was accordingly believed that, even if he did put an end to himself with a sword, his wound was cured, and his life preserved, according to that which was written regarding him—'And his mortal wound was healed,' [Revelation 13:3]—to be sent forth again near the end of the world, in order that he may practice the mystery of iniquity."

CHAPTER III

After an interval of some years from the death of Nero, there arose another tyrant no less wicked (Domitian) who, although his government was exceedingly odious, for a very long time oppressed his subjects and reigned in security, until at length he stretched forth his impious hands against the Lord.[1] Having been instigated by evil demons to persecute the righteous people, he was then delivered into the power of his enemies and suffered due punishment. To be murdered in his own palace was not vengeance ample enough: the very memory of his name was erased. For although he had erected many admirable edifices, and rebuilt the Capitol, and left other distinguished marks of his magnificence, yet the senate did so persecute his name, as to leave no remains of his statues, or traces of the inscriptions put up in honor of him, and by most solemn and severe decrees it branded him, even after death, with perpetual infamy.

Thus, the commands of the tyrant having been rescinded, the Church was not only restored to her former state, but she shone forth with additional splendor, and became more and more flourishing. And in the times that followed, while many well-deserving princes guided the helm of the Roman Empire, the Church suffered no violent assaults from her enemies, and she extended her hands unto the east and unto the west, insomuch that now there was not even a remote corner of the earth to which the divine religion had not penetrated, or any nation of manners so barbarous that did not, by being converted to the worship of God, become mild and gentle.[2]

NOTES

1. Domitian, the son of Vespasian and brother of Titus, reigned from AD 81 to AD 96. His connection to the persecution of Christians in contemporary sources is rather tenuous and seems to have been restricted to Rome itself, having subjected a number of Christians to banishment. Saint John the Evangelist seems to have been exiled to the island of Patmos during his reign. Similarly, we find Domitian's niece, Domitilla, banished to the island of Pandateria, while her husband Flavius Clemens, and the ex-consul Glabrio were slain for supposedly adopting "Jewish ways" and atheism according to the 3rd century historian, Dio Cassius. See *Roman History*, epitome of Book LXVII. The charge of atheism was commonly made against Christians who refused to recognize the Roman pantheon. In the 19th century, the archaeologist Giovanni de Rossi demonstrated that this Domitilla owned a villa in Rome that was later used as a Christian burial ground as early as the 1st century AD. See the entry for Flavia Domitilla in *The Catholic Encyclopedia*, 1909 edition.

2. Lactantius here ignores persecution incidents which may have taken place during the years between the death of Domitian and the reign of Decius. These include the deaths of such famous martyrs as Polycarp, Ignatius of Antioch, Justin Martyr, and numerous others. It is clear from the well-attested correspondence between Trajan and Pliny the Younger, that Christians remained subject to legal prosecution including capital punishment during all or some of this period. However, most of the incidents which took place at this time were highly localized and seemed to focus on one or a

6

few individuals. For the correspondence in question, see Williams, *Pliny: Correspondence with Trajan from Bithynia, Epistles X, 15–121*.

CHAPTER IV

This long peace, however, was afterwards interrupted. Decius appeared in the world, an accursed wild beast, to afflict the Church, and who but a bad man would persecute religion?[1] It seems as if he had been raised to sovereign eminence at once to rage against God and at once to fall. For having undertaken an expedition against the Carpi, who had then possessed themselves of Dacia and Mœsia, he was suddenly surrounded by the barbarians and slain together with a great part of his army.[2] Nor could he be honored with the rites of sepulture but, stripped and naked, he lay to be devoured by wild beasts and birds—a fit end for the enemy of God.[3]

NOTES

1. Decius reigned from AD 249 to 251. His well-attested persecution of Christians is considered the first organized, empire-wide effort to extirpate Christianity from the Roman dominions. Records of the Decian persecution may be found in Christian hagiographical literature from the time, including the *Life and Passion of Saint Cyprian* by Pontius the Deacon, and the epistles of Saint Cyprian, who was sent into exile during this period. During this time, Christians were made to sacrifice publicly to the pagan pantheon and obtain a formal certificate, called a *libellus*, stating that they had done so. More information and samples of these may be found in Knipfing, "The Libelli of the Decian Persecution," in *The Harvard Theological Review*, Vol. 16, No. 4, pages 345–390.

2. The events leading up to the death of Decius may be found described in the *Gothic History* of Jordanes. This source is an abridgement of a much larger Gothic history written by Cassiodorus in the early 6th century, which is itself drawn from much earlier sources. In it, Jordanes describes how Decius's son was slain while fighting against the Goths under king Cniva. Decius rode out to Abrittus in Mœsia

and sought either vengeance for his son or death. He and his men were cut off by the Goths and slain. See Jordanes, Chapter XVIII.

3.   This passage hearkens to Jeremiah 22:19 and 36:30.

CHAPTER V

And presently Valerian also, in a mood alike frantic, lifted up his impious hands to assault God and, although his time was short, shed much righteous blood.[1] But God punished him in a new and extraordinary manner, that it might be a lesson to future ages that the adversaries of Heaven always receive the just recompense of their iniquities. He, having been made prisoner by the Persians, lost not only that power which he had exercised without moderation, but also the liberty of which be had deprived others. And he wasted the remainder of his days in the vilest condition of slavery. For Sapores,[2] the king of the Persians, who had made him prisoner, whenever he chose to get into his carriage or to mount on horseback, commanded the Roman to stoop and present his back.

Then, setting his foot on the shoulders of Valerian, he said with a smile of reproach, "This is true, and not what the Romans delineate on board or plaster." Valerian lived for a considerable time under the well-merited insults of his conqueror, so that the Roman name remained long the scoff and derision of the barbarians. And this also was added to the severity of his punishment, that although he had an emperor for his son, he found no one to revenge his captivity and most abject and servile state. Neither indeed was he ever demanded back.

Afterward, when he had finished this shameful life under so great dishonor, he was flayed and his skin, stripped from the flesh, was dyed with vermilion and placed in the temple of the gods of the barbarians, that the remembrance of a triumph so signal might be perpetuated, and that this spectacle might always be exhibited to our ambassadors as an admonition to the Romans that, beholding the spoils of their captive emperor in a Persian temple, they should not place too great confidence in their own strength.[3]

Now since God so punished the sacrilegious, is it not strange that any one should afterward have dared to do, or even to devise, aught against the majesty of the one God, who governs and supports all things?

NOTES

1. Valerian ruled from AD 253 through AD 260 and launched a persecution similar in scope to that of Decius. For this period, we may again refer to the *Life and Passion of Saint Cyprian*, who met his end during this persecution. Also executed during this persecution were well-known martyrs in Rome such as Saint Lawrence and Pope Saint Sixtus II, as well as the Spanish martyr Saint Fructuosus and his companions. For a full account, see Healy, *The Valerian Persecution.*

2. This refers to Shapur I, King of Persia, who ruled from ca. AD 241 through AD 270, a time of almost continual conflict between Persia and the Roman Empire.

3. Regarding the end of Valerian, the existing ancient historical sources vary in their reports. Eutropius, writing about a hundred years after the event, says that Valerian was captured following a defeat and reduced to servitude among the Persians. See *Breviarium*, Book IX, Chapter 7. Conversely, Zosimus, who wrote in the early 6th century though clearly drawing from much earlier sources, claims that Valerian had embarked on a peace mission to Shapur when he was treacherously captured. See *New History*, Book I:36. A monumental stone relief in Naqš-e Rustam, Iran, shows Shapur I on horseback receiving the submission of a Roman emperor, presumed to be Valerian.

CHAPTER VI

Aurelian might have recollected the fate of the captive Valerian, yet being of a nature outrageous and headstrong, he forgot both his sin and its punishment, and by deeds of cruelty irritated the divine wrath.[1] He was not, however, permitted to accomplish what he had devised.[2] For just as he began to give a loose to his rage, he was slain. His bloody edicts had not yet reached the more distant provinces, when he himself lay all bloody on the earth at Cænophrurium in Thrace, assassinated by his familiar friends, who had taken up groundless suspicions against him.[3]

Examples of such a nature, and so numerous, ought to have deterred succeeding tyrants. Nevertheless they were not only not dismayed but, in their misdeeds against God, became more bold and presumptuous.

NOTES

1. Aurelian ruled the empire from AD 270 through AD 275. His reign began at the climax of the crisis of the 3rd century when both the Gallic Empire in the West and the Empire of Palmyra in the East became independent realms separate from Roman authority. Aurelian defeated both of these polities and reintegrated them into the Roman Empire, while at the same time defeating various barbarian incursions into the empire. He is perhaps best known for encircling the city of Rome with the monumental walls named after him, remnants of which survive to this day. In celebration of his achievements, he was deemed *Restitutor Orbis*—restorer of the world.

2. Corroborating this story is the testimony of Eusebius in his *Ecclesiastical History*, who claims that Aurelian was moved to take action against the Christians late in his reign due to evil counsel he had received, and indeed, the edicts were about to be signed when Aurelian was slain. See Eusebius, *Ecclesiastical History*, Book VII, Chapter 30. For an alternative view of Aurelian's status as a persecutor, see Hurley, "Some Thoughts on the Emperor Aurelian as 'Persecutor.'" in *The Classical World*, Vol. 106, No. 1, pages 75–89.

3. A more detailed account of Aurelian's death may be found in Eutropius who says that one of the emperor's slaves produced a forged document purporting to be a list of the emperor's allies in the military who he intended to put to death. When this document was produced before these men, they took matters into their own hands and slew Aurelian first. See *Breviarium*, Book IX, Chapter 15.

CHAPTER VII

While Diocletian,[1] that author of ill and deviser of misery, was ruining all things, he could not withhold his insults, not even against God. This man, by avarice partly, and partly by timid counsels, overturned the Roman Empire. For he made choice of three persons to share the government with him, and thus, the empire having been quartered, armies were multiplied and each of the four princes strove to maintain a much more considerable military force than any sole emperor had done in times past.[2] There began to be fewer men who paid taxes than there were who received wages, so that the means of the husbandmen being exhausted by enormous impositions, the farms were abandoned, cultivated grounds became woodland, and universal dismay prevailed. Besides, the provinces were divided into minute portions, and many presidents and a multitude of inferior officers lay heavy on each territory and almost on each city. There were also many stewards of different degrees and deputies of presidents. Very few civil causes came before them, but there were condemnations daily, and forfeitures frequently inflicted, taxes on numberless commodities, and those not only often repeated but perpetual and, in exacting them, intolerable wrongs.

Whatever was laid on for the maintenance of the soldiery might have been endured. But Diocletian, through his insatiable avarice, would never allow the sums of money in his treasury to be diminished. He was constantly heaping together extraordinary aids and free gifts, that his original hoards might remain untouched and inviolable. He also, when by various extortions he had made all things exceedingly dear, attempted by an ordinance to limit their prices.[3] Then much blood was shed for the veriest trifles.

Men were afraid to expose anything to sale, and the scarcity became more excessive and grievous than ever until in the end, the ordinance after having proved destructive to multitudes, was from mere necessity abrogated.

To this there was added a certain endless passion for building, and on that account, endless exactions from the provinces for furnishing wages to laborers and artificers, and supplying carriages and whatever else was requisite to the works which he projected: here public halls, there a circus, here a mint, and there a workhouse for making implements of war. In one place a habitation for his empress, and in another for his daughter. Presently a great part of the city was quitted, and all men removed with their wives and children, as from a town taken by enemies. And when those buildings were completed, to the destruction of whole provinces, he said, "They are not right. Let them be done on another plan." Then they were to be pulled down, or altered, to undergo perhaps a future demolition. By such folly was he continually endeavoring to equal Nicomedia with the city of Rome in magnificence.[4]

I omit mentioning how many perished on account of their possessions or wealth, for such evils were exceedingly frequent, and through their frequency appeared almost lawful. But this was peculiar to him: that whenever he saw a field remarkably well cultivated or a house of uncommon elegance, a false accusation and a capital punishment were straightway prepared against the proprietor, so that it seemed as if Diocletian could not be guilty of rapine without also shedding blood.

NOTES

1. Lactantius here introduces Diocletian, who was born of humble parentage in Dalmatia and originally called by the name Diocles. His ability as a soldier and leader was recognized by the barracks

emperors of the mid-3rd century, and he rose steadily through the ranks. He eventually became a close associate of the emperor Carus, attaining the rank of *Comes Domesticorum* and the consulship. Upon the death of Carus while on campaign in Persia, Diocletian was able to gain control of the empire after the death of Carus's two sons, Carinus and Numerian. Diocletian reigned from AD 284 until his resignation from the imperial authority in AD 305. A great reformer, it was he who devised the system of the Tetrarchy which remained in force during the time of Lactantius's literary activity. He was also the emperor ultimately responsible for the Great Persecution of Christians which persisted from AD 303 through AD 311. *On the Deaths of the Persecutors* is one of the most important primary sources for the reign of Diocletian. For a thorough modern biography of the man and his reign, see Williams, *Diocletian and the Roman Recovery.*

2. This refers to the first Tetrarchy which was composed of the senior Augusti, Diocletian and Maximian, and the junior Cæsars, Galerius and Constantius. Diocletian and Galerius jointly ruled the East while Maximian and Constantius ruled the West.

3. Diocletian's edict on maximum prices still exists, at least in part. For a translation and commentary, see Graser, "A text and translation of the Edict of Diocletian," in T. Frank (ed.), *An Economic Survey of Ancient Rome Volume V: Rome and Italy of the Empire*.

4. Diocletian ruled from Nicomedia in Bithynia.

CHAPTER VIII

What was the character of his brother in empire, Maximian, called Herculius?[1] Not unlike to that of Diocletian, and indeed, to render their friendship so close and faithful as it was, there must have been in them a sameness of inclinations and purposes, a corresponding will and unanimity in judgment. Herein alone they were different, that Diocletian was more avaricious and less resolute, and that Maximian, with less avarice, had a bolder spirit, prone not to good but to evil. For while he possessed Italy, itself the chief seat of empire, and while other very opulent provinces such as Africa and Spain were near at hand, he took little care to preserve those treasures which he had such fair opportunities of amassing. Whenever he stood in need of more, the richest senators were presently charged, by suborned evidences, as guilty of aspiring to the empire so that the chief luminaries of the senate were daily extinguished. And thus the treasury, delighting in blood, overflowed with ill-gotten wealth.

Add to all this the incontinency of that pestilent wretch, not only in debauching males which is hateful and abominable, but also in the violation of the daughters of the principal men of the state. For wherever he journeyed, virgins were suddenly torn from the presence of their parents. In such enormities he placed his supreme delight, and to indulge to the utmost his lust and flagitious desires was, in his judgment, the felicity of his reign.

I pass over Constantius, a prince unlike the others and worthy to have had the sole government of the empire.[2]

NOTES

1. Maximian, whose full name was M. Aurelius Valerius Maximianus, was of humble origins having been born in Pannonia. He rose through the ranks of the army and achieved repute such that Diocletian saw fit to make him first Cæsar in AD 285 and his colleague as Augustus in AD 286. At the same time, Diocletian bestowed upon him the name Herculius while Diocletian himself took the name Jovius, an indication of the patron deities which the Augusti invoked to protect their reigns. Maximianus would go on to rule the West as senior emperor until forced to resign along with Diocletian in AD 305. Much of what we know about his life and his reign is due to the present work of Lactantius.
2. Here Lactantius refers to Constantius I, the father of Constantine the Great. As with Maximian and Diocletian, Constantius was born in the Balkan provinces and made a name for himself in the Roman army during the crisis of the late 3rd century. He would be chosen by Diocletian and Maximian to become Cæsar or junior emperor of the West in AD 293 and would distinguish himself by reclaiming Britain for the empire and defending the Gallic frontiers. He would reign as Augustus of the West from the abdication of Maximian in AD 305 until his death a year later.

CHAPTER IX

But the other Maximian (Galerius), chosen by Diocletian for his son-in-law, was worse, not only than those two princes whom our own times have experienced, but worse than all the bad princes of former days.[1] In this wild beast there dwelt a native barbarity and a savageness foreign to Roman blood—and no wonder, for his mother was born beyond the Danube, and it was an inroad of the Carpi that obliged her to cross over and take refuge in New Dacia. The form of Galerius corresponded with his manners. Of stature tall, full of flesh, and swollen to a horrible bulk of corpulency. By his speech, gestures, and looks, he made himself a terror to all that came near him. His father-in-law, too, dreaded him excessively. The cause was this.

Narseus, king of the Persians, emulating the example set him by his grandfather Sapores, assembled a great army and aimed at becoming master of the eastern provinces of the Roman Empire.[2] Diocletian, apt to be low-spirited and timorous in every commotion and fearing a fate like that of Valerian, would not in person encounter Narseus. But he sent Galerius by the way of Armenia, while he himself halted in the eastern provinces and anxiously watched the event. It is a custom amongst the barbarians to take everything that belongs to them into the field. Galerius laid an ambush for them and easily overthrew men embarrassed with the multitude of their followers and with their baggage. Having put Narseus to flight and returned with much spoil, his own pride and Diocletian's fears were greatly increased. For after this victory he rose to such a pitch of haughtiness as to reject the appellation of Cæsar, and when he heard that appellation in letters addressed to him, he cried out with a stern look and terrible voice, "How long am I to be Cæsar?"

Then he began to act extravagantly insomuch that, as if he had been a second Romulus, he wished to pass for and to be called the offspring of Mars. And that he might appear the issue of a divinity, he was willing that his mother Romula should be dishonored with the name of adulteress. But not to confound the chronological order of events, I delay the recital of his actions. For indeed afterwards, when Galerius got the title of emperor, his father-in-law having been divested of the imperial purple, he became altogether outrageous and of unbounded arrogance.

While by such a conduct and with such associates, Diocles—for that was the name of Diocletian before he attained sovereignty—occupied himself in subverting the commonweal, there was no evil which his crimes did not deserve. Nevertheless he reigned most prosperously, as long as he forbore to defile his hands with the blood of the just. And what cause he had for persecuting them, I come now to explain.

NOTES

1. Finally, Lactantius introduces the man who is perhaps the greatest villain of *On the Deaths of the Persecutors*, Galerius Valerius Maximianus. Lactantius often refers to him as "the other Maximian." For the sake of clarity, he is called Galerius throughout this translation. As with the three other members of the Tetrarchy, Galerius was born in the Balkan provinces, probably as indicated by Lactantius, of a barbarian mother. Aurelius Victor says that his parents were cattle herders and therefore gives Galerius the cognomen Armentarius or "herdsman." See *De Cæsaribus*, Chapter 40. He rose through the ranks of the army to reach a position where he would be elevated to serve as Cæsar of the East under Diocletian at about the same time as Constantius. In this role he proved proficient at defending the empire's frontiers. Following the abdication of Diocletian, he would go on to become the Augustus of the East after AD 305 until his death in AD 311. Though highly biased against Galerius, Lactantius provides much of the detail for what we know about the reign of this emperor, who is portrayed as the

primary motivator behind the Great Persecution and several other key events during this period.

2. Narses or Narseh succeeded to the throne of Persia in AD 293 after toppling the weak Vahram III. According to Eutropius, Galerius's first campaign against Narses resulted in a humiliating defeat for Roman arms, and upon his return to Diocletian, the Augustus forced his defeated Cæsar to run beside his chariot for several miles while still wearing his scarlet robes. See *Breviarium* Book IX, Chapter 24–25. Galerius would get his revenge a few years later, decisively defeating Narses and successfully settling relations with the Sassanid Persian kingdom for several decades. For more about the wars between Galerius and Narses, see: Southern, *The Roman Empire from Severus to Constantine*, page 232.

CHAPTER X

Diocletian, as being of a timorous disposition, was a searcher into futurity, and during his abode in the East he began to slay victims that from their livers he might obtain a prognostic of events.[1] And while he sacrificed, some attendants of his who were Christians stood by and they put the immortal sign on their foreheads. At this the demons were chased away and the holy rites interrupted.[2] The soothsayers trembled, unable to investigate the wonted marks on the entrails of the victims. They frequently repeated the sacrifices, as if the former had been unpropitious, but the victims, slain from time to time, afforded no tokens for divination. At length Tages, the chief of the soothsayers, either from guess or from his own observation, said, "There are profane persons here who obstruct the rites."[3]

Then Diocletian, in furious passion, ordered not only all who were assisting at the holy ceremonies but also all who resided within the palace to sacrifice, and in case of their refusal, to be scourged. And further, by letters to the commanding officers, he enjoined that all soldiers should be forced to the like impiety, under pain of being dismissed from the service.[4] Thus far his rage proceeded, but at that season he did nothing more against the law and religion of God. After an interval of some time he went to winter in Bithynia, and presently Galerius Cæsar came thither, inflamed with furious resentment and purposing to excite the inconsiderate old man to carry on that persecution which he had begun against the Christians. I have learned that the cause of his fury was as follows.

NOTES

1. This refers to the Roman pagan practice of divination known as haruspices.
2. Other examples of the pagan rituals being disrupted by the presence of Christians or Christian symbols may be found in literature from this period. See, for example, the *Ecclesiastical History* of Hermias Sozomen (Book V, Chapter 2) who recounts how Julian the Apostate, when participating in a pagan ritual, accidentally signed himself with the cross by force of habit thereby disrupting the rites.
3. According to ancient Roman legend, Tages was a divine being who emerged from the ground in Etruria and taught the Etruscans to practice the haruspices.
4. Eusebius Pamphilus mentions in his *Ecclesiastical History* that the persecution, "began with the brethren in the army." See Book VIII, Chapter 1.

CHAPTER XI

The mother of Galerius, a woman exceedingly superstitious, was a votary of the gods of the mountains.[1] Being of such a character, she made sacrifices almost every day and she feasted her servants on the meat offered to idols. But the Christians of her family would not partake of those entertainments, and while she feasted with the Gentiles, they continued in fasting and prayer. On this account she conceived ill-will against the Christians, and by woman-like complaints instigated her son, no less superstitious than herself, to destroy them.

So, during the whole winter, Diocletian and Galerius held councils together at which no one else assisted. And it was the universal opinion that their conferences respected the most momentous affairs of the empire. The old man long opposed the fury of Galerius, and showed how pernicious it would be to raise disturbances throughout the world and to shed so much blood, saying that the Christians were wont with eagerness to meet death and that it would be enough for him to exclude persons of that religion from the court and the army. Yet he could not restrain the madness of that obstinate man. He resolved, therefore, to take the opinion of his friends. Now this was a circumstance in the bad disposition of Diocletian, that whenever he determined to do good, he did it without advice so that the praise might be all his own. But whenever he determined to do ill, which he was sensible would be blamed, he called in many advisers so that his own fault might be imputed to other men.[2] And therefore a few civil magistrates and a few military commanders were admitted to give their counsel, and the question was put to them according to priority of rank. Some, through personal ill-will towards the Christians, were of the opinion that they ought to be cut off as enemies of the gods and adversaries of the established religious ceremonies. Others thought differently, but having understood the will of Galerius, they, either from dread of displeasing or from a desire of gratifying him, concurred in the opinion given against the Christians.[3]

Yet not even then could the emperor be prevailed upon to yield his assent. He determined above all to consult his gods, and to that end he dispatched a soothsayer to inquire of Apollo at Miletus whose answer was such as might be expected from an enemy of the divine religion. So Diocletian was drawn over from his purpose. But although he could struggle no longer against his friends, and against

Cæsar and Apollo, yet still he attempted to observe such moderation as to command the business to be carried through without bloodshed, whereas Galerius would have had all persons burnt alive who refused to sacrifice.

NOTES

1. The mother of Galerius was named Romula as Lactantius mentioned in Chapter IX.

2. This passage provides an historical framework for the conferences which took place at Nicomedia leading up to the Great Persecution. This framework, the personalities involved, and the arguments in play, are explored in much greater detail in *The Making of a Christian Empire: Lactantius and Rome* by Elizabeth DePalma Digeser.

3. Lactantius seems to have been an eye-witness to these events taking place in Nicomedia during his tenure there. In his *Divine Institutes* (Book V, Chapters 2–3), he calls out an anonymous philosopher and a government official as the producers of anti-Christian works that instigated the persecution. These are identified by Digeser in *The Making of a Christian Empire* as Porphyry of Tyre and Sossianus Hierocles. Lactantius claims that these men were the primary public apologists for the persecution in Nicomedia, stating that both had, "set forth their sacrilegious writings in my presence."

CHAPTER XII

A fit and auspicious day was sought out for the accomplishment of this undertaking, and the festival of the god Terminus, celebrated on the sevens of the kalends of March, was chosen in preference to all others to terminate, as it were, the Christian religion.[1]

"That day, the harbinger of death, arose,
First cause of ill, and long enduring woes"[2]

which befell not only the Christians, but the whole earth. When that day dawned, in the eighth consulship of Diocletian and seventh of Maximian, suddenly while it was yet hardly light, the prefect together with chief commanders, tribunes, and officers of the treasury, came to the church in Nicomedia, and the gates having been forced open, they searched everywhere for an image of the Divinity. The books of the Holy Scriptures were found and they were committed to the flames. The utensils and furniture of the church were abandoned to pillage: all was rapine, confusion, tumult. That church, situated on rising ground, was within view of the palace, and Diocletian and Galerius stood, as if on a watch-tower, disputing long whether it ought to be set on fire. The sentiment of Diocletian prevailed, who dreaded lest so great a fire being once kindled, some part of the city might he burnt, for there were many and large buildings that surrounded the church. Then the Prætorian Guards came in battle array with axes and other iron instruments, and having been let loose everywhere, they in a few hours levelled that very lofty edifice with the ground.[3]

NOTES

1. That is, February 23, AD 303. Eusebius gives the date of the beginning of the persecution as March of 303 near the time of Easter. This discrepancy can be explained by assuming that word of the initiation of the persecution would have reached Eusebius somewhat later than Lactantius who was at the epicenter of imperial power at Nicomedia.

2. Lactantius quotes here Virgil's *Æneid,* Book IV:169–170—the passage foreshadowing the long sequence of woes brought about by the illicit union of Æneas and Dido. For more on Lactantius's use of quotations from Virgil and the Sibylline Books, see Christensen: *Lactantius the Historian*, pages 33 and following.

   It should be noted that during this time, Virgil was considered by some Christians to be a pre-Christian prophet. His words were called out as such by no less than Constantine himself in his Oration to the Saints, wherein he quotes Virgil's Fourth Eclogue. See *Oration of Constantine Which He Addressed to the Assembly of the Saints*, Chapter 19–21 in Schaff and Wace. *Nicene and Post-Nicene Fathers: Second Series, Volume 1: Eusebius, Church History, Life of Constantine the Great, and Oration in Praise of Constantine.*

3. Lactantius likely would have been an eyewitness to this event and gives the only detailed description extant. Eusebius confirms that the destruction of churches was part of Diocletian and Galerius's program of persecution. See *Ecclesiastical History*, Book VIII, Chapter 2.

CHAPTER XIII

The next day an edict was published depriving the Christians of all honors and dignities, ordaining also that without any distinction of rank or degree they should be subjected to tortures, and that every suit at law should be received against them, while on the other hand, they were debarred from being plaintiffs in questions of wrong, adultery, or theft, and finally, that they should neither be able to live in freedom, nor have any voice.[1]

A certain person tore down this edict and cut it in pieces, improperly indeed but with high spirit, saying in scorn, "These are the triumphs of Goths and Sarmatians." Having been instantly seized and brought to judgment, he was not only tortured but roasted alive in the forms of law, and having displayed admirable patience under sufferings, he was consumed to ashes.[2]

NOTES

1. Compare this to the litany of punishments given by Eusebius in his *Ecclesiastical History,* Book VIII, Chapter 2.
2. The same story is told by Eusebius in *Ecclesiastical History*, Book VIII, Chapter 5, who supplies some additional details, calling the man who tore down the edict, "not obscure but very highly honored with distinguished temporal dignities." This anonymous martyr has been occasionally identified with Saint George, but more modern scholars identify him as Evethius, a name that is mentioned in the Syriac Martyrology of AD 411 in connection with Nicomedia. See Woods, D. 2008. "Pope Zacharias and the Head of Saint George," in *ARAM Periodical,* Vol. 20, page 164, fn 4.

CHAPTER XIV

But Galerius, not satisfied with the tenor of the edict, sought in another way to gain on the emperor. That he might urge him to excess of cruelty in persecution, he employed private emissaries to set the palace on fire, and some part of it having been burnt, the blame was laid on the Christians as public enemies.[1] And the very appellation of Christian grew odious on account of that fire. It was said that the Christians, in concert with the eunuchs, had plotted to destroy the princes, and that both of the princes had well-nigh been burnt alive in their own palace. Diocletian, shrewd and intelligent as he always chose to appear, suspected nothing of the contrivance, but inflamed with anger, immediately commanded that all his own domestics should be tortured to force a confession of the plot. He sat on his tribunal, and saw innocent men tormented by fire to make discovery.[2] All magistrates and all who had superintendency in the imperial palace obtained special commissions to administer the torture, and they strove with each other who should be first in bringing to light the conspiracy. No circumstances, however, of the fact were detected anywhere, for no one applied the torture to any domestics of Galerius. He himself was ever with Diocletian, constantly urging him and never allowing the passions of the inconsiderate old man to cool.

Then, after an interval of fifteen days, he attempted a second fire. But that was perceived quickly and extinguished. Still, however, its author remained unknown. On that very day, Galerius, who in the middle of winter had prepared for his departure, suddenly hurried out of the city, protesting that he fled to escape being burnt alive.[3]

NOTES

1. Eusebius also records this fire at the palace, confirming that the blame for it was placed on the Christians. Like Lactantius, he avers that the accusation is false though Lactantius is unique in accusing Galerius of using the conflagration as a false flag. See Eusebius, *Ecclesiastical History,* Book VIII, Chapter 6. Constantine, who was also present in Nicomedia at the time, claims that the fire was started by a lightning strike and that Diocletian's private chambers were destroyed. See *Oration of Constantine to the Assembly of the Saints* in *A Select Library of Nicene and Post-Nicene Fathers of the Christian Church, Volume I: Eusebius,* Chapter XXV.

2. Eusebius gives the name of three martyrs among those who served in the imperial palace, specifically Dorotheus, Gorgonius and Peter, though he says that "many others of the royal household, after varied sufferings, ended their lives by strangling." See *Ecclesiastical History*, Book VIII, Chapter 6.

3. Lactantius is the only source to record the second fire.

CHAPTER XV

And now Diocletian raged not only against his own domestics but indiscriminately against all, and he began by forcing his daughter Valeria and his wife Prisca to be polluted by sacrificing.[1] Eunuchs, once the most powerful and who had chief authority at court and with the emperor, were slain. Presbyters and other officers of the Church were seized without evidence by witnesses or confession, condemned, and together with their families led to execution.[2] In burning alive, no distinction of sex or age was regarded, and because of their great multitude, they were not burnt one after another, but a herd of them were encircled with the same fire. And servants, having millstones tied about their necks, were cast into the sea.

Nor was the persecution less grievous on the rest of the people of God, for the judges, dispersed through all the temples, sought to compel everyone to sacrifice. The prisons were crowded. Tortures, hitherto unheard of were invented. And lest justice should be inadvertently administered to a Christian, altars were placed in the courts of justice hard by the tribunal, that every litigant might offer incense before his cause could be heard. Thus judges were no otherwise approached than as divinities.

Mandates also had gone to Maximian Herculius and Constantius requiring their concurrence in the execution of the edicts, for in matters even of such mighty importance their opinion was never once asked. Herculius, a person of no merciful temper, yielded ready obedience and enforced the edicts throughout his dominions of Italy. Constantius, on the other hand, lest he should have seemed to dissent from the injunctions of his superiors, permitted the demolition of churches—mere walls, and capable of being built up again—but he preserved entire that true temple of God, which is the human body.[3]

NOTES

1. Lactantius is the only contemporary source to record these details of Diocletian's family. The implication here is that Diocletian's wife, Prisca, and his daughter, Valeria, the wife of Galerius, were secret Christians. If this were true, it would not be surprising that a large number of Christians resided in the palace among the domestic servants of the two women prior to the persecution. It might also help explain the source of the enmity that Galerius conceived toward the Christian religion, given the Cæsar's Bacchanalian lifestyle as compared to the moral strictures enjoined by Christianity. The pathetic fates of these women is recorded later in this narrative. See Chapters XXXIX–XLI and LI.

2. Eusebius mentions that Anthimius, the bishop of Nicomedia, was beheaded at the time of the fire in the palace, and that a great multitude of others in the city were subsequently killed. See *Ecclesiastical History*, Book VIII, Chapter 6.

3. Here Lactantius draws the distinction between the behavior of the zealous persecutors (Diocletian, Galerius and Maximian) and the reluctant persecutor (Constantius), no doubt as a nod to his own

imperial patron, Constantine. And while this is an obvious attempt by Lactantius to excuse the father of Constantine for his actions during the Great Persecution, it also serves as clear evidence that the persecutory edicts were enforced empire-wide.

CHAPTER XVI

Thus was all the earth afflicted, and from east to west, except in the territories of Gaul, three ravenous wild beasts continued to rage.

"Had I a hundred mouths, a hundred tongues,
A voice of brass, and adamantine lungs,
Not half the dreadful scene could I disclose,"[1]

or recount the punishments inflicted by the rulers in every province on religious and innocent men.

But what need of a particular recital of those things, especially to you, my best beloved Donatus, who above all others was exposed to the storm of that violent persecution? For when you had fallen into the hands of the prefect Flaccinus, no puny murderer,[2] and afterwards of Hierocles, who from a deputy became president of Bithynia, the author and adviser of the persecution,[3] and last of all into the hands of his successor Priscillian,[4] you displayed to mankind a pattern of invincible magnanimity. Having been nine times exposed to racks and diversified torments, nine times by a glorious profession of your faith you foiled the adversary. In nine combats you subdued the devil and his chosen soldiers, and by nine victories you triumphed over this world and its terrors. How pleasing the spectacle to God, when He beheld you a conqueror, yoking in your chariot not white horses, nor enormous elephants, but those very men who had led captive the nations! After this sort to lord it over the lords of the earth is triumph indeed! Now, by your valor were they conquered when you set at defiance their flagitious edicts, and through steadfast faith and the fortitude of your soul, you routed all the vain terrors of tyrannical authority. Against you neither scourges, nor iron claws, nor fire, nor sword, nor various kinds of torture availed aught. And no violence could bereave you of your fidelity and persevering resolution. This it is to be a disciple of God, and this it is to be a soldier of Christ—a soldier whom no enemy can dislodge or wolf snatch from the heavenly camp, no artifice ensnare or pain of body subdue or torments overthrow.

At length, after those nine glorious combats, in which the devil was vanquished by you, he dared not to enter the lists again with one whom, by repeated trials, he had found unconquerable. And he abstained from challenging you anymore, lest you should have laid hold on the garland of victory already stretched out to you—an unfading garland, which although you have not at present received it, is laid up in the kingdom of the Lord for your virtue and deserts.[5]

But let us now return to the course of our narrative.

NOTES

1. Lactantius quotes here a passage from Virgil's *Æneid,* Book VI: 625–627 in which the Cumean Sibyl enumerates the crimes and punishments of those condemned to Tartarus.
2. Flaccinus is not otherwise known from any other source.
3. This is, no doubt, Sossianus Hierocles who is mentioned in Chapter XI, note 3.
4. Priscillian is also otherwise unknown to history.
5. By surviving the tortures without abjuring his faith, Donatus is considered a confessor, not a martyr.

CHAPTER XVII

The wicked plan having been carried into execution, Diocletian, whom prosperity had now abandoned, set out instantly for Rome, there to celebrate the commencement of the twentieth year of his reign. That solemnity was performed on the twelfth of the kalends of December.[1] And suddenly the emperor, unable to bear the Roman freedom of speech, peevishly and impatiently burst away from the city. The kalends of January approached at which day the consulship for the ninth time was to be offered to him.[2] Yet, rather than continue thirteen days longer in Rome, he chose that his first appearance as consul should be at Ravenna.[3] Having, however, begun his journey in winter amidst intense cold and incessant rains, he contracted a slight but lingering disease. It harassed him without intermission, so that he was obliged for the most part to be carried in a litter. Then, at the close of summer, he made a circuit along the banks of the Danube and so came to Nicomedia. His disease had now become more grievous and oppressing, yet he caused himself to be brought out in order to dedicate that circus which at the conclusion of the twentieth year of his reign he had erected. Immediately he grew so languid and feeble, that prayers for his life were put up to all the gods.

Then suddenly on the ides of December,[4] there was heard in the palace sorrow, and weeping, and lamentation, and the courtiers ran to and fro. There was silence throughout the city, and a report went of the death and even of the burial of Diocletian. But early on the morrow it was suddenly rumored that he still lived. At this the countenance of his domestics and courtiers changed from melancholy to gay. Nevertheless there were those who suspected his death to be kept secret until the arrival of Galerius Cæsar, lest in the meanwhile the soldiery should attempt some change in the government. And this suspicion grew so universal, that no one would believe the emperor alive until on the kalends of March,[5] he appeared in public but so wan, his illness having lasted almost a year, as hardly to be known again. The fit of stupor, resembling death, happened on the ides

28

of December and although he in some measure recovered, yet he never attained to perfect health again, for he became disordered in his judgment, being at certain times insane and at others of sound mind.

NOTES

1. That is, November 20, AD 303. On that date began the Vicennalia or 20th year of Diocletian's reign.
2. January 1, which is also the day that a new consular term began.
3. This was most likely Diocletian's only visit to Rome during his tenure as emperor. According to Eutropius, this visit corresponded with a joint celebration of a triumph by him and Maximian which included a display of the sisters, wives, and children of the defeated Persian king, Narses, as mentioned in Chapter IX, note 2. See *Breviarium*, Book IX, Chapter 27. Some additional details are provided by the *Chronography of Filocalus of AD 354* which says that Diocletian and Maximian "scattered gold and silver coins in the circus." Possibly as a result of this, a retaining wall in the circus collapsed and 13,000 were killed. This awful tragedy no doubt threw a pall over the triumph and was perhaps what spurred the Romans to speak out against Diocletian, causing the latter's hasty withdrawal from the city.
4. December 13, AD 304.
5. March 1, AD 305.

CHAPTER XVIII

Within a few days Galerius Cæsar arrived, not to congratulate his father-in-law on the re-establishment of his health, but to force him to resign the empire. Already he had urged Maximian Herculius to the like purpose and by the alarm of civil wars terrified the old man into compliance. And he now assailed Diocletian. At first, in gentle and friendly terms, he said that age and growing infirmities disabled Diocletian for the charge of the commonweal, and that he had need to give himself some repose after his labors. Galerius, in confirmation of his argument, produced the example of Nerva, who laid the weight of empire on Trajan.[1]

But Diocletian made answer that it was unfit for one who had held a rank eminent above all others and conspicuous to sink into the obscurity of a low station. Neither indeed was it safe because in the course of so long a reign he must unavoidably have made many enemies. The case of Nerva was very different. He, after having reigned a single year, felt himself, either from age or from inexperience in business, unequal to affairs so momentous and therefore threw aside the helm of government and returned to that private life in which he had already grown old. But Diocletian added, that if Galerius wished for the title of emperor, there was nothing to hinder its being conferred on him and Constantius, as well as on Maximian Herculius.

Galerius, whose imagination already grasped at the whole empire, saw that little but an unsubstantial name would accrue to him from this proposal and therefore replied that the settlement made by Diocletian himself ought to be inviolable—a settlement which provided that there should be two of higher rank vested with supreme power, and two others of inferior to assist them. Easily might concord be preserved between two equals, never amongst four; that he, if Diocletian would not resign, must consult his own interests so as to remain no longer in an inferior rank, and the last of that rank; that for fifteen years past he had been confined as an exile to Illyricum and the banks of the Danube, perpetually struggling against barbarous nations, while others at their ease governed dominions more extensive than his and better civilized.

Diocletian already knew by letters from Maximian Herculius all that Galerius had spoken at their conference and also that he was augmenting his army. And now, on hearing his discourse, the spiritless old man burst into tears and said, "Be it as you will."

It remained to choose Cæsars by common consent. "But," said Galerius, "why ask the advice of Maximian and Constantius, since they must needs acquiesce in whatever we do?"

"Certainly they will," replied Diocletian, "for we must elect their sons."

Now Maximian Herculius had a son, Maxentius, married to the daughter of Galerius, a man of bad and mischievous dispositions and so proud and stubborn withal, that he would never pay the wonted obeisance either to his father or father-in-law, and on that account he was hated by them both. Constantius also had a son, Constantine, a young man of very great worth and well meriting the high station of Cæsar. The distinguished comeliness of his figure, his strict attention to all military duties, his virtuous demeanor and singular affability, had endeared him to the troops and made him the choice of every individual. He was then at court, having long before been created by Diocletian a tribune of the first order.

"What is to be done?" said Galerius, "for that Maxentius deserves not the office. He who, while yet a private man, has treated me with contumely, how will he act when once he obtains power?"

"But Constantine is amiable, and will so rule as hereafter in the opinion of mankind to surpass the mild virtues of his father."

"Be it so, if my inclinations and judgment are to be disregarded. Men ought to be appointed who are at my disposal, who will dread me and never do anything unless by my orders."

"Whom then shall we appoint?"

"Severus."[2]

"What! That dancer, that habitual drunkard who turns

night into day and day into night?"

"He deserves the office, for he has proved himself a faithful paymaster and purveyor of the army. And, indeed, I have already dispatched him to receive the purple from the hands of Maximian."

"Well, I consent, but whom else do you suggest?"

"Him," said Galerius, pointing out Daia, a young man, half-barbarian. Now Galerius had lately bestowed part of his own name on that youth and called him Maximin, in like manner as Diocletian formerly bestowed on Galerius the name of Maximian, for the omen's sake because Maximian Herculius had served him with unshaken fidelity.[3]

"Who is that you present?"

"A kinsman of mine."

"Alas!" said Diocletian, heaving a deep sigh, "you do not propose men fit for the charge of public affairs!"

"I have tried them."

"Then do you look to it, who are about to assume the administration of the empire. As for me, while I continued emperor, long and diligent have been my labors in providing for the security of the commonweal and now, should anything disastrous ensue, the blame will not be mine."[4]

NOTES

1. The abdication of Diocletian and Maximian was such a momentous event that it was described in numerous other sources including Eutropius who considers the retirement an act worthy of praise. See *Breviarium,* Book IX, Chapter 28. The anonymous Latin panegyricist of AD 310 portrayed the abdication as pre-planned by Diocletian and Maximian and not the result of pressure from Galerius. See Nixon, *In Praise of the Later Roman Emperors*, page 202–203. Aurelius Victor claims that Diocletian was given an augury of an imminent plunge of the empire's fortunes and abdicated the imperial power in anticipation, convincing Maximian, with great difficulty, to do likewise. See *De Cæsaribus,* Chapter 39. Of these, Lactantius was the closest to the events in terms of both time and place.

2. Flavius Valerius Severus is introduced in this dialogue. Practically all we know about Severus and his brief reign comes from Lactantius. His status as low-born and "given to drink" is confirmed by Anonymous Valesianus, Part I, Chapter IV.

3. Galerius Valerius Maximinus Daia, known more commonly as Maximin Daia, was of Illyrian peasant origin like his uncle, Galerius. Aurelius Victor calls him Daca and says that he was born into a shepherd family (similar to Galerius) but that he was mild of temper and a promoter of learned men and literature. He allows, however, that Maximin over-indulged in drink, again similar to his uncle. See *De Cæsaribus*, Chapter 40. Maximin would go on to become a ferocious persecutor of Christians, rivaling his uncle in this regard. Many aspects of his life as Cæsar and Augustus are known to us exclusively from Lactantius in the following chapters. For a full and detailed biography of Maximin, see Christensen, *C. Galerius Valerius Maximinus: Studies in the Politics and Religion of the Roman Empire, AD 305–313*.

4. This extraordinary dialogue is recorded nowhere else. While it is difficult to believe that Lactantius could have heard the words verbatim from the mouths of Diocletian and Galerius, the tenor of the dialogue seems to offer a legitimate explanation for why the tetrarchy evolved in such an unexpected way.

CHAPTER XIX

Matters having been thus concerted, Diocletian and Galerius went in procession to publish the nomination of the Cæsars. Everyone looked at Constantine, for there was no doubt that the choice would fall on him. The troops present, as well as the chief soldiers of the other legions who had been summoned to the solemnity, fixed their eyes on Constantine, exulted in the hope of his approaching election, and occupied themselves in prayers for his prosperity.

Near three miles from Nicomedia there is an eminence, on the summit of which Galerius formerly received the purple. And there a pillar with the statue of Jupiter was placed. Thither the procession went. An assembly of the soldiers was called. Diocletian, with tears, harangued them and said that he had become infirm, that he needed repose after his fatigues, and that he would resign the empire into hands more vigorous and able and, at the same time, appoint new Cæsars.

The spectators, with the utmost earnestness, waited for the nomination. Suddenly he declared that the Cæsars were Severus and Maximin. The amazement was universal. Constantine stood near in public view, and men began to question amongst themselves whether his name too had not been changed into Maximin—when, in the sight of all, Galerius, stretching back his hand, put Constantine aside and drew Daia forward, and having divested him of the garb of a private person, set him in the most conspicuous place. All men wondered who he could be and from whence he came, but none ventured to interpose or move objections, so confounded were their minds at the strange and unlooked-for event.[1]

Diocletian took off his purple robe, put it on Daia, and resumed his own original name of Diocles. He descended from the tribunal and passed through Nicomedia in a chariot, and then this old emperor, like a veteran soldier freed from military service, was dismissed into his own country.[2] Meanwhile Daia, lately taken from the tending of cattle in forests to serve as a common soldier, immediately made one of the lifeguard, presently a tribune, and next day Cæsar, obtained authority to trample under foot and oppress the empire of the East—a person ignorant alike of war and of civil affairs, and from a herdsman become a leader of armies.[3]

NOTES

1. This extraordinary narrative is the only extant account of this momentous event whereby Diocletian formally resigned as emperor and raised two relative unknowns, Severus and Maximin Daia, as Cæsars. Given the position of Lactantius and his likely presence in

Nicomedia at this time, he could very well have been an eyewitness to the event. However, it should be kept in mind that by the time he is writing *On the Deaths of the Persecutors*, he was already part of Constantine's court. Therefore, this account is likely tinged with Constantinian propaganda.

2. Diocletian would retire to the Dalmatian coast where he was born, residing at a palace-fortress near the city of Salona at modern-day Split, Croatia. He is later re-introduced by Lactantius in Chapter XLI and following in connection with the fate of his wife and daughter.

3. Lactantius's description of Maximin as of low birth from a shepherd family is supported by Aurelius Victor. See above, Chapter XVIII, note 3.

CHAPTER XX

Galerius, having effected the expulsion of the two old men, began to consider himself alone as the sovereign of the Roman Empire. Necessity had required the appointment of Constantius to the first rank, but Galerius made small account of one who was of an easy temper and of declining and precarious health. He looked for the speedy death of Constantius. And although that prince should recover, it seemed not difficult to force him to put off the imperial purple, for what else could he do if pressed by his three colleagues to abdicate? Galerius had Licinius ever about his person, his old and intimate acquaintance and his earliest companion in arms whose counsels he used in the management of all affairs.[1] Yet he would not nominate Licinius to the dignity of Cæsar with the title of son, for he purposed to nominate him in the room of Constantius to the dignity of emperor with the title of brother, while he himself might hold sovereign authority and rule over the whole globe with unbounded licence.[2] After that, he meant to have solemnized the vicennial festival, to have conferred on his son Candidianus, then a boy of nine years of age, the office of Cæsar[3] and, in conclusion, to have resigned as Diocletian had done. And thus, Licinius and Severus being emperors and Maximin and Candidianus in the next station of Cæsars, he fancied that environed as it were by an impregnable wall, he should lead an old age of security and peace. Such were his projects, but God, whom he had made his adversary, frustrated all those imaginations.

NOTES

1. This is the first mention by Lactantius of the enigmatic figure of Valerius Licinianus Licinius who would go on to become the final and most dangerous rival of Constantine. It should be kept in mind that the rivalry between Constantine and Licinius for preeminence in the Roman Empire happened largely after the publication of *On the Deaths of the Persecutors*. Indeed, the present work was almost certainly written during a period of concord between the two emperors, cemented by the marriage of Licinius to Constantine's sister, Constantia. It is worth noting, however, that introducing Licinius as an old comrade of the arch-persecutor Galerius can hardly be considered flattering. Eutropius confirms Licinius's background as a partisan of Galerius and mentions that he came to the Cæsar's attention for his vigorous efforts during his war against King Narses in Persia. See *Breviarium*, Book X, Chapter 4. Aurelius Victor offers a somewhat longer description of Licinius's character, calling him greedy, licentious and ignorant, while at the same time friendly toward the farmers from whose ranks he was sprung. He also upheld the traditions of the army and attempted to suppress some of the oriental practices introduced by Diocletian, calling the palace eunuchs, "vermin." See *De Cæsaribus*, Chapter 41.

2. This strategy of promoting Licinius above the head of the existing Cæsar would later arouse the wrath of Maximin Daia. See below, Chapter XXXII.

3. Practically all we know about Candidianus comes from the present work.

CHAPTER XXI

Having thus attained to the highest power, he bent his mind to afflict that empire into which he had opened his way. It is the manner and practice of the Persians for the people to yield themselves slaves to their kings and for the kings to treat their people as slaves. This villainous man, from the time of his victories over the Persians, was not ashamed incessantly to extol such an institution, and he resolved to establish it in the Roman dominions.[1] And because he could not do this by an express law, he so acted in imitation of the Persian kings as to bereave men of their liberties. He first of all degraded those whom he meant to punish, and then not only were inferior magistrates put to the torture by him but also the chief men in cities and persons of the most eminent rank, and this too in matters of little moment and in civil questions. Crucifixion was the punishment readily prepared in capital cases, and for lesser crimes, fetters. Matrons of honorable station were dragged into workhouses, and when any man was to be scourged, there were four posts fixed in the ground, and to them he was tied after a manner unknown in the chastisement of slaves.

What shall I say of his enjoyment of sport and of his favorite diversions? He kept bears, most resembling himself in fierceness and bulk, whom he had collected together during the course of his reign. As often as he chose to indulge his humor, he ordered some particular bear to be brought in, and men were thrown to that savage animal rather to be swallowed up than devoured. And when their limbs were torn asunder, he laughed with excessive complacency: nor did he ever sup without being spectator of the effusion of human blood.[2]

Men of private station were condemned to be burnt alive, and he began this mode of execution by edicts against the Christians, commanding that after torture and condemnation, they should be burnt at a slow fire.[3] They were fixed to a stake and first a moderate flame was applied to the soles of their feet until the muscles, contracted by burning, were torn from the bones. Then torches, lighted and put out again, were directed to all the members of their bodies so that no part had any exemption. Meanwhile cold water was continually poured on their faces, and their mouths moistened, lest by reason of their jaws being parched, they should expire. At length they did expire when, after many hours, the violent heat had consumed their skin and penetrated into their intestines. The dead carcasses were laid on a funeral pile and wholly burnt. Their bones were gathered, ground to powder, and thrown into the river or into the sea.[4]

NOTES

1. The introduction of oriental practices into the Roman imperial system of government is normally ascribed to Diocletian. These practices included prostration when entering the semi-divine imperial presence, calling the emperor *Dominus* (Lord), the proliferation of eunuchs among the imperial court, and a general degradation of traditional Roman offices of state and the role of the senatorial elite. In part as a result of these changes, scholars often refer to this period of Roman history as the Dominate. It is noteworthy that Lactantius considers the barbaric Galerius in part responsible for these changes that were so alien to traditional Roman practice. For an in depth discussion of Lactantius's attitude toward the Dominate and the Principate which preceded it, as well as the complex religious and philosophical questions underpinning the shift, see Digeser: *The Making of a Christian Empire*.

2. Condemnation *ad bestias* was a common form of capital punishment used throughout Roman history for criminals who were slaves, foreigners or members of the lower social classes. Included among the *summa supplicia* (ultimate punishments), condemnation via the beasts was often reserved for the worst types of offenders. Christians had been considered part of this class of offenders since at least the time of Nero. For a more detailed discussion of Roman capital punishment, see Kyle: *Spectacles of Death in Ancient Rome*, page 53 and following.

3. Condemnation *ad flammas* was another of the *summa supplicia* utilized by the Romans for criminals of the worst types. As with condemnation *ad bestias*, death by burning had been used against Christians since the persecution of Nero who, apparently, sentenced the Christians of Rome to be torn by wild beasts as well as burned

as just retribution for their supposed crime of arson. See *Annals* of Tacitus, Book 15, Chapter 44. Given that Galerius had accused Christians of attempting to burn the imperial palace at Nicomedia, he may have had a similar aim in mind when condemning Christians to the flames.

4. The complete destruction of the condemned Christian's body following execution was a response to the common practice of gathering up and venerating relics of slain martyrs by the Christian faithful. See *The Ecclesiastical History* of Eusebius, Book VIII, Chapter 6, where he notes that the bodies of the Christians from the imperial palace who were among the first executed in Nicomedia were exhumed and thrown into the sea, lest they become objects of veneration.

CHAPTER XXII

And now that cruelty which he had learned in torturing the Christians became habitual, and he exercised it against all men indiscriminately. He was not wont to inflict the slighter sorts of punishment, as to banish, to imprison, or to send criminals to work in the mines. But to burn, to crucify, to expose to wild beasts were things done daily and without hesitation. For smaller offenses, those of his own household and his stewards were chastised with lances instead of rods. And, in great offences, to be beheaded was an indulgence shown to very few, and it seemed as a favor, on account of old services, when one was permitted to die in the easiest manner.[1]

But these were slight evils in the government of Galerius, when compared with what follows. For eloquence was extinguished, pleaders cut off, and the learned in the laws either exiled or slain. Useful letters came to be viewed in the same light as magical and forbidden arts, and all who possessed them were trampled upon and execrated as if they had been hostile to government and public enemies. Law was dissolved and unbounded licence permitted to judges—to judges chosen from amongst the soldiery, rude and illiterate men and let loose upon the provinces—without assessors to guide or control them.[2]

NOTES

1. This seems to be another example of Lactantius rebuking Galerius for resorting to some very un-Roman, semi-barbaric practices, namely subjecting Roman citizens of even the highest classes to the most severe forms of punishment available under the law, even for petty offenses.
2. For Romans, a complex and just system of laws was a hallmark of the highest civilization, whereas rulers who acted outside the law, disregarded the forms or behaved capriciously according to their own wills were considered tyrants akin to barbarian kings.

CHAPTER XXIII

But that which gave rise to public and universal calamity was the tax imposed at once on each province and city. Surveyors having been spread abroad and occupied in a general and severe scrutiny, horrible scenes were exhibited, like the outrages of victorious enemies and the wretched state of captives. Each spot of ground was measured, vines and fruit-trees numbered, lists taken of animals of every kind, and a capitation-roll made up. In cities, the common people, whether residing within or without the walls, were assembled. The market-places were filled with crowds of families, all attended with their children and slaves, and the noise of torture and scourges resounded. Sons were hung on the rack to force discovery of the effects of their fathers, the most trusty slaves compelled by pain to bear witness against their masters, and wives to bear witness against their husbands. In default of all other evidence, men were tortured to speak against themselves, and no sooner did agony oblige them to acknowledge what they had not, but those imaginary effects were noted down in the lists. Neither youth, nor old age, nor sickness afforded any exemption. The diseased and the infirm were carried in, the age of each was estimated and, that the capitation-tax might be enlarged, years were added to the young and struck off from the old. General lamentation and sorrow prevailed. Whatever, by the laws of war, conquerors had done to the conquered, the like did this man presume to perpetrate against Romans and the subjects of Rome,[1] because his forefathers had been made liable to a like tax imposed by the victorious Trajan as a penalty on the Dacians for their frequent rebellions.

After this, money was levied for each head, as if a price had been paid for liberty to exist. Yet full trust was not reposed on the same set of surveyors, but others and others still were sent round to make further discoveries. And thus the tributes were redoubled, not because the new surveyors made any fresh discoveries, but because they added at pleasure to the former rates lest they should seem to have been employed to no purpose. Meanwhile the number of animals decreased and men died—nevertheless taxes were paid even for the dead, so that no one could either live or cease to live without being subject to impositions.

There remained mendicants alone from whom nothing could be exacted and whom their misery and wretchedness secured from ill-treatment. But this pious man had compassion on them, and determining that they should remain no longer in indigence, he caused them all to be assembled, put on board vessels, and sunk in the sea. So merciful was he in making provision that under his administration no man should want! And thus, while he took effectual measures that none under the feigned pretext of poverty should elude the tax, he put to death a multitude of real wretches in violation of every law of humanity.[2]

NOTES

1. Thus Galerius treats his own subjects like a conquered enemy. This passage harkens back to the famous passage in Livy describing the capitulation of the Romans to Brennus the Gaul in 387 BC. Brennus attempted to extort an even greater payment than had been agreed upon for the Gauls to depart from the environs of Rome. When the Romans protested, Brennus offered a mocking rejoinder which Livy describes as hateful to Roman ears: "Woe to the conquered." See *The History of Rome*, Book V, Chapter 48.

2. For a very detailed exploration of the program of taxation under Diocletian and Galerius, as well as an examination of Lactantius's own view that the reform of the system of taxation resulted in greater injustice and a divided Roman society, see Clark: *Taxation and the Formation of the Late Roman Social Contract,* page 73 and following.

CHAPTER XXIV

Already the judgment of God approached him and that season ensued in which his fortunes began to droop and to waste away. While occupied in the manner that I have described above, he did not set himself to subvert or expel Constantius, but waited for his death not imagining, however, that it was so nigh. Constantius, having become exceedingly ill, wrote to Galerius and requested that his son Constantine might be sent to see him. He had made a like request long before but in vain, for Galerius meant nothing less than to grant it. On the contrary, he laid repeated snares for the life of that young man because he dared not use open violence lest he should stir up civil wars against himself and incur that which he most dreaded—the hate and resentment of the army. Under pretence of manly exercise and recreation, he made him combat with wild beasts, but this device was frustrated. For the power of God protected Constantine, and in the very moment of jeopardy rescued him from the hands of Galerius.[1]

At length, Galerius, when he could no longer avoid complying with the request of Constantius, one evening gave Constantine a warrant to depart and commanded him to set out next morning with the imperial despatches. Galerius meant either to find some pretext for detaining Constantine or to forward orders to Severus for arresting him on the road. Constantine discerned his purpose and therefore, after supper when the emperor was gone to rest, he hasted away, carried off from the principal stages all the horses maintained at the public expense, and escaped. Next day the emperor, having purposely remained in his bed-chamber until noon, ordered Constantine to be called into his presence. But he learnt that Constantine had set out immediately after supper. Outrageous with passion, he ordered horses to be made ready, that Constantine might be pursued and dragged back. And hearing that all the horses had been carried off from the great road, he could hardly refrain from tears.[2]

Meanwhile Constantine, journeying with incredible rapidity, reached his father who was already about to expire.[3] Constantius recommended his son to the soldiers, delivered the sovereign authority into his hands, and then died as his wish had long been in peace and quiet.[4] Constantine Augustus, having assumed the government, made it his first care to restore the Christians to the exercise of their worship and to their God, and so began his administration by reinstating the holy religion.[5]

NOTES

1. Numerous other ancient sources confirm Constantine's presence at the eastern court in Nicomedia, including Eusebius in his *Life of the Blessed Emperor Constantine*, Book I, Chapters 12, 19, and 20. Eusebius's account of events generally agrees with Lactantius. Several other sources detail the snares set by Galerius for Constantine. Anonymous Valesianus mentions Constantine doing battle against the Sarmatians and leading his troops through

a swamp at the order of Galerius (Part I, Chapter 2). In the epitome of Praxagoras's *History of Constantine the Great*, Galerius had Constantine do battle with a lion. After killing the beast, Constantine decided to flee to his father. Praxagoras's original work is lost, but an epitome of it may be found in the so-called *Library* of Photius (1920 edition), page 62.

2. Constantine's flight from the east to be with his father before the latter's death is confirmed by numerous other ancient sources with varying levels of detail. Eusebius, of course, mentions it in *Life of the Blessed Emperor Constantine* (Book I, Chapter XX). In the account reported by Anonymous Valesianus, Constantine killed all of the post-horses in order to throw off any pursuers.

3. Most of the ancient sources agree with the sense of Lactantius that Constantine arrived just in time to witness his father's death. See, in particular, Eusebius's *Life of the Blessed Emperor Constantine*, Book I, Chapter XXI. However, in two other sources, a rather different sequence of events unfolds. Anonymous Valesianus Part I, Chapter 2, reports that Constantine caught up with his father at Bononia (modern day Boulogne-sur-mer in France) and the two crossed into Britain together. They then proceeded to win a victory over the Picts, after which Constantius perished in July of AD 306 at Eboracum (modern day York in the UK). The Latin Panegyric of AD 310, appears to confirm this, saying that Constantine arrived, "at the very time your father was crossing the sea to Britain." See Nixon: *In Praise of Later Roman Emperors: The Panegyrici Latini*, page 228. It is likely, however, that Constantius was already very ill when Constantine arrived and declined in health as the year progressed. Lactantius is likely compressing the timeframe for dramatic effect.

4. The raising of Constantine to the imperial authority by his father's wish and by the acclamation of his father's army complicated the Tetrarchic system, though clearly if Galerius, in his role as Cæsar, could advocate for the abdication of the senior Augusti and nominate new Cæsars, then certainly Constantius had the right to do likewise. Lactantius indicates, however, that Constantine was acclaimed as Augustus, not merely as Cæsar. As we shall see in the next chapter, Constantine will accept demotion to the rank of Cæsar, for a year at least, while Severus assumed the role of Augustus of the west. Nevertheless, this situation may be seen as the beginning of the breakdown of the Tetrarchic system which would decline even more precipitously with the elevation of Maxentius later in AD 306. See Chapter XXVI.

5. Some scholars have suggested that this passage may indicate that Constantine rebuilt the churches that were previously destroyed by

his father as mentioned in Chapter XV. See Barnes, "Lactantius and Constantine," in *Journal of Roman Studies*, Vol. 63, page 46.

CHAPTER XXV

Some few days after, the portrait of Constantine adorned with laurels was brought to the pernicious wild beast,[1] that by receiving that symbol he might acknowledge Constantine in the quality of emperor. He hesitated long whether to receive it or not, and he was about to commit both the portrait and its bearer to the flames, but his confidants dissuaded him from a resolution so frantic. They admonished him of the danger, and they represented that if Constantine came with an armed force, all the soldiers, against whose inclination obscure or unknown Cæsars had been created, would acknowledge him and crowd eagerly to his standard. So Galerius, although with the utmost unwillingness, accepted the portrait and sent the imperial purple to Constantine, that he might seem of his own accord to have received that prince into partnership of power with him.

And now his plans were deranged and he could not, as he intended formerly, admit Licinius without exceeding the limited number of emperors. But this he devised: that Severus, who was more advanced in life, should be named emperor,[2] and that Constantine, instead of the title of emperor to which he had been named, should receive that of Cæsar in common with Maximin Daia, and so be degraded from the second place to the fourth.

NOTES

1. That is, Galerius.
2. In other words, Galerius proposed that Severus, who had been Cæsar or junior emperor of the West, be promoted to Augustus of the West, while Constantine, who had been named Augustus of the West by his father's troops outside of the regular order, be demoted

to Cæsar. Constantine accepted this arrangement as it re-enforced his legitimacy. Thus, as of AD 306, the Tetrarchy consisted of Galerius and Maximin Daia in the East, Severus and Constantine in the West.

CHAPTER XXVI

Things seemed to be arranged in some measure to the satisfaction of Galerius when another alarm was brought— that his son-in-law Maxentius had been declared emperor at Rome.[1] The cause was this: Galerius having resolved by permanent taxes to devour the empire, soared to such extravagance in folly as not to allow an exemption from that thralldom even to the Roman people. Tax-gatherers therefore were appointed to go to Rome and make out lists of the citizens.[2] Much about the same time Galerius had reduced the Prætorian Guards. There remained at Rome a few soldiers of that body who, profiting of the opportunity, put some magistrates to death and with the acquiescence of the tumultuary populace, clothed Maxentius in the imperial purple.

Galerius, on receiving this news, was disturbed at the strangeness of the event but not much dismayed. He hated Maxentius and he could not bestow on him the dignity of Cæsar already enjoyed by two (Daia and Constantine). Besides, he thought it enough for him to have once bestowed that dignity against his inclination. So he sent for Severus, exhorted him to regain his dominion and sovereignty, and he put under his command that army which Maximian Herculius had formerly commanded that he might attack Maxentius at Rome. There the soldiers of Maximian had been oftentimes received with every sort of luxurious accommodation, so that they were not only interested to preserve the city, but they also longed to fix their residence in it.

Maxentius well knew the enormity of his own offences, although he had as it were an hereditary claim to the services of his father's army and might have hoped to draw it over to himself. Yet he reflected that this consideration might occur to Galerius also and induce him to leave Severus in Illyricum and march in person with his own army against Rome. Under such apprehensions, Maxentius sought to protect himself from the danger that hung over him. To his father, who since his abdication resided in Campania, he sent the purple and saluted him again Augustus. Maximian, given to change, eagerly resumed that purple of which he had unwillingly divested himself.[3]

Meanwhile Severus marched on and with his troops approached the walls of the city. Presently the soldiers raised up their ensigns, abandoned Severus, and yielded themselves to Maxentius against whom they had come. What remained but flight for Severus, thus deserted? He was encountered by Maximian, who had resumed the imperial dignity. On this he took refuge in Ravenna, and shut himself up there with a few soldiers. But perceiving that he was about to be delivered up, he voluntarily surrendered himself and restored the purple to him from whom he had received it. And after this he obtained no other grace but that of an easy death, for he was compelled to open his veins and in that gentle manner expired.[4]

NOTES

1. Marcus Aurelius Valerius Maxentius was the son of the retired Augustus of the West, Maximian Herculius, and his wife Eutropia. He was the brother of Fausta who would become the second wife of Constantine in AD 307. The pagan historian Zosimus, writing in the early 6th century, gives the most detailed account of Maxentius's attempt at imperial power saying that he became incensed at the good fortune of Constantine and therefore plotted with two tribunes of the Prætorian Guard and a swine merchant to seize power. He names the tribunes Marcellianus and Marcellus, and the swine

merchant Lucianus. As part of the plot, the conspirators assassinated Abellius, the prefect of Rome, and made a substantial donative to those who aided in his enterprise. See *New History*, Book II:9.

2. Rome was traditionally exempt from taxation which explains why the novelty of tax collectors appearing in Rome would have prompted such an extreme reaction. Evidence from the *Theodosian Code* demonstrates that Rome remained exempt from taxation even long after this event. See Book XI, Title 20:3.

3. Zosimus provides an alternative story, namely, that Maximian came out of retirement on his own accord. See *New History*, Book II:10.

4. Anonymous Valesianus offers additional details, saying that Maximian provided oaths of safety to Severus and thereby fooled him into leaving Ravenna and coming to Rome. Severus was captured by forces loyal to Maxentius at a place called Tre Tabernae. He was then held as a captive until Galerius entered Italy, at which point he was executed. See Part I, Chapter 4. Zosimus says that Severus was executed immediately after his capture. See *New History*, Book II:10.

CHAPTER XXVII

But Maximian, who knew the outrageous temper of Galerius, began to consider that, fired with rage on hearing of the death of Severus, he would march into Italy and that possibly he might be joined by Daia, and so bring into the field forces too powerful to be resisted. Having therefore fortified Rome and made diligent provision for a defensive war, Maximian went into Gaul, that he might give his younger daughter Fausta in marriage to Constantine and thus win over that prince to his interest.[1]

Meantime Galerius assembled his troops, invaded Italy, and advanced towards Rome, resolving to extinguish the senate and put the whole people to the sword. But he found everything shut and fortified against him. There was no hope of carrying the place by storm, and to besiege it was an arduous undertaking, for Galerius had not brought with him an army sufficient to invest the walls.[2] Probably, having never seen Rome, he imagined it to be little superior in size to those cities with which he was acquainted. But some of his legions, detesting the wicked enterprise of a father against his son-in-law, and of Romans against Rome, renounced his authority and carried over their ensigns to the enemy. Already had his remaining soldiers begun to waver, when Galerius, dreading a fate like that of Severus and having his haughty spirit broken and humiliated, threw himself at the feet of his soldiers, and continued to beseech them that he might not be delivered to the foe until by the promise of mighty largesses, he prevailed on them.[3]

Then he retreated from Rome and fled in great disorder. Easily might he have been cut off in his flight had any one pursued him even with a small body of troops. He was aware of his danger and allowed his soldiers to disperse themselves and to plunder and destroy far and wide that if there were any pursuers, they might be deprived of all means of subsistence. So the parts of Italy through which that pestilent band took its course were wasted, all things pillaged, matrons forced, virgins violated, parents and husbands compelled by torture to disclose where they had concealed their goods, and their wives and daughters. Flocks and herds of cattle were driven off like spoils taken from barbarians. And thus did he, once a Roman emperor, but now the ravager of Italy, retire into his own territories after having afflicted all men indiscriminately with the calamities of war.[4] Long ago, indeed, and at the very time of his obtaining sovereign power, he had avowed himself the enemy of the Roman name, and he proposed that the empire should be called, not the Roman, but the Dacian empire.

NOTES

1. Constantine and Fausta were married in AD 307. She would bear him three sons, Constantine II, Constans, and Constantius II,

all three of whom would go on to become emperors in their own right. Previous to his marriage to Fausta, Constantine had a relationship with a woman named Minervina who bore him a son named Crispus, probably while he was still in the East. Little is known about Minervina and even her name is only revealed by Zosimus writing nearly two centuries later. A pagan with an animus toward Constantine, Zosimus calls Minervina a concubine. See *New History*, Book II:20. Later scholars have upgraded Minervina's status to Constantine's first wife and suggested that she had already died by the time Constantine married Fausta. See Odahl, *Constantine and the Christian Empire*, page 72.

2. Galerius is certainly not the only general in history to experience difficulties besieging the enormous city of Rome. Hannibal never made the attempt even after his stunning victory at Cannae during the Second Punic War. Alaric had to besiege Rome twice before taking the city by treachery in AD 410. The Gothic king Vittiges would prove unable to take the city even though he outnumbered the defenders about twenty-to-one during the Gothic wars of the late 530s.

3. This is the most detailed extant account of Galerius's ill-fated campaign against Maxentius. Anonymous Valesianus offers a few additional details, including that Galerius sent Licinius and Probus into Rome to parley with Maxentius, but their mission failed as Maxentius became confident of luring away Galerius's troops as he had those of Severus before. See Part I, Chapter 3.

4. Anonymous Valesianus confirms that Galerius allowed his men to plunder everything along the Via Flaminia, which ran from Rome east to Ariminum (modern Rimini) on the Adriatic Sea during the course of his retreat. See Part I, Chapter 3.

CHAPTER XXVIII

After the flight of Galerius, Maximian, having returned from Gaul, held authority in common with his son, but more obedience was yielded to the young man than to the old. For Maxentius had more power and had been longer in possession of it, and it was to him that Maximian owed on this occasion the imperial dignity. The old man was impatient at being denied the exercise of uncontrolled sovereignty and envied his son with a childish spirit of rivalry, and therefore he began to consider how he might expel Maxentius and resume his ancient dominion. This appeared easy because the soldiers who deserted Severus had originally served in his own army. He called an assembly of the people of Rome and of the soldiers, as if he had been to make an harangue on the calamitous situation of public affairs. After having spoken much on that subject, he stretched his hands towards his son, charged him as author of all ills and prime cause of the calamities of the state, and then tore the purple from his shoulders. Maxentius, thus stripped, leaped headlong from the tribunal and was received into the arms of the soldiers.[1] Their rage and clamor confounded the unnatural old man and, like another Tarquin the Proud, he was driven from Rome.[2]

NOTES

1. Lactantius is the only extant source for these interesting details on the falling out of Maximian and Maxentius.
2. Tarquinius Superbus, or Tarquin the Proud, was the last king of pre-Republican Rome. He was deposed by a revolution of the people in 510 BC which ushered in the Roman Republic. It is noteworthy that Tarquin had usurped the throne via intrigue, his wife Tullia having helped him overthrow and assassinate her own father, King Servius Tullius. Tarquin's reign was signalized by conspiracy, deception, double-dealing, intra-familial conspiracy, and sexual excesses which, no doubt, made him an attractive parallel to Maximian for Lactantius.

CHAPTER XXIX

Then Maximian returned into Gaul, and after having made some stay in those quarters, he went to Galerius, the enemy of his son, that they might confer together, as he pretended, about the settlement of the commonweal. But his true purpose was, under color of reconciliation, to find an opportunity of murdering Galerius and of seizing his share of the empire instead of his own from which he had been everywhere excluded.

Diocles was at the court of Galerius when Maximian arrived, for Galerius, meaning now to invest Licinius with the ensigns of supreme power in the place of Severus, had lately sent for Diocles to be present at the solemnity.[1] So it was performed in presence both of him and of Maximian, and thus there were six who ruled the empire at one and the same time.[2]

Now the designs of Maximian having been frustrated, he took flight as he had done twice before and returned into Gaul with a heart full of wickedness, intending by treacherous devices to overreach Constantine who was not only his own son-in-law, but also the child of his son-in-law.[3] And that he might the more successfully deceive, he laid aside the imperial purple. The Franks had taken up arms. Maximian advised the unsuspecting Constantine not to lead all his troops against them, and he said that a few soldiers would suffice to subdue those barbarians. He gave this advice that an army might be left for him to win over to himself, and that Constantine, by reason of his scanty forces, might be overpowered.

The young prince believed the advice to be judicious because it was given by an aged and experienced commander, and he followed it because it was given by a father-in-law. He marched, leaving the most considerable part of his forces behind. Maximian waited a few days, and as soon as, by his calculation, Constantine had entered the territory of the barbarians, he suddenly resumed the imperial purple, seized the public treasures, after his wont made ample donatives to the soldiery, and feigned that such disasters had befallen Constantine as soon after befell himself.[4] Constantine was presently informed of those events, and by marches astonishingly rapid, he flew back with his army. Maximian, not yet prepared to oppose him, was caught unawares and overpowered, and the soldiers returned to their duty.

Maximian had possessed himself of Marseilles (he fled thither) and shut the gates. Constantine drew nigh, and seeing Maximian on the walls, addressed him in no harsh or hostile language and demanded what he meant, and what it was that he wanted, and why he had acted in a way so peculiarly unbecoming him. But Maximian from the walls incessantly uttered abuse and curses against Constantine. Then, of a sudden, the gates on the opposite side having been unbarred, the besiegers were admitted into the city.[5] The rebel emperor and unnatural parent and a perfidious father-in-law was dragged into the presence of Constantine, heard a recital made of his crimes, was divested of his imperial robe, and after this reprimand, obtained his life.

NOTES

1. This is the so-called Conference of Carnuntum. According to Eutropius, upon the rise of Maxentius, Maximian left his place of retirement and wrote letters to Diocletian encouraging the old man to resume the imperial authority. Diocletian, says Eutropius, disregarded these pleas. See *Breviarium*, Book X, Chapter 2. Zosimus offers a few additional details, saying that at the conference in Carnuntum, Maximian again exhorted Diocletian to reassume the imperial power to save the government which they had established from falling into ruin. Diocletian refused, preferring to remain in his quiet life of retirement. See *New History*, Book II:10. Aurelius Victor adds a quote of Diocletian who, when asked to resume the purple by Maximian and Galerius, replied, "If you could only see the cabbages raised by our hands at Salonae, you would surely never judge that a temptation." See *De Cæsaribus*, Chapter 39.

2. The six rulers in question at this time are Galerius and Maximin Daia in the East, and Licinius, Constantine, Maxentius and Maximian in the West.

3. Lactantius says this because Constantine was the husband of Maximian's daughter, Fausta, as well as the step-son of Maximian's other daughter, Theodora, who had married Constantine's father,

Constantius I, when he was made Cæsar in AD 293. Most scholarly sources consider Fausta and Theodora to be half-sisters, the actual parentage of Theodora being somewhat confused. For additional details, see Odahl: *Constantine and the Christian Empire*, page 48 and page 320, note 21.

4. This rebellion of Maximian is covered in some detail by the anonymous author of the Panegyric of AD 310 who says that Constantine was engaged in building a bridge over the Rhine at Cologne when he received news that Maximian had revolted. See Nixon: *In Praise of Later Roman Emperors: The Panegyrici Latini*, page 237.

5. The Panegyricist of AD 310 includes additional details on the movements of Maximian and Constantine during this time. See Nixon: *In Praise of Later Roman Emperors: The Panegyrici Latini*, pages 243 and following.

CHAPTER XXX

Maximian, having thus forfeited the respect due to an emperor and a father-in-law, grew impatient at his abased condition and, emboldened by impunity, formed new plots against Constantine. He addressed himself to his daughter Fausta and, as well by entreaties as by the soothing of flattery, solicited her to betray her husband. He promised to obtain for her a more honorable alliance than that with Constantine, and he requested her to allow the bed-chamber of the emperor to be left open and to be slightly guarded.

Fausta undertook to do whatever he asked and instantly revealed the whole to her husband. A plan was laid for detecting Maximian in the very execution of his crime. They placed a base eunuch to be murdered instead of the emperor. At the dead of night Maximian arose and perceived all things to be favorable for his insidious purpose. There were few soldiers on guard, and these too at some distance from the bed-chamber. However, to prevent suspicion, he accosted them and said that he had had a dream which he wished to communicate to his son-in-law. He went in armed, slew the eunuch, sprung forth exultingly and avowed the murder. At that moment Constantine showed himself on the opposite side with a band of soldiers. The dead body was brought out of the bedchamber.[1] The murderer, taken in the fact, all aghast,

"Stood like a stone, silent and motionless,"[2]

while Constantine upbraided him for his impiety and enormous guilt. At last Maximian obtained leave for the manner of his death,

"and from a high beam, he tied the knot for his foul demise."[3]

Thus that mightiest sovereign of Rome—who ruled so long with exceeding glory and who celebrated his twentieth anniversary—thus that most haughty man had his neck broken and ended his detestable life by a death base and ignominious.[4]

NOTES

1. This account of Maximian's assassination attempt against Constantine is by far the most detailed extant. Other accounts, such as that of Eusebius in his *Life of the Blessed Emperor Constantine*, Book I, Chapter 47, speak only of a treasonous conspiracy. Eutropius confirms that Fausta revealed her father's treachery to her husband. See *Breviarium*, Book X, Chapter 3.
2. This quote is from Virgil, *Æneid*, Book VI, line 471 and refers to the reaction of the shade of Dido to the sorrowful words of Æneas when he meets her in the underworld.
3. Here is another quote from the *Æneid*, Book XII, line 603, wherein Virgil describes the death of Amata, queen consort of Latinus. Fearing her cause lost and feeling guilt at being the instigator of a miserable war, Amata hung herself.
4. Aurelius Victor agrees that Maximian died "having his neck snapped by a noose," but does not include the detail that Maximian apparently did the deed himself. See *De Cæsaribus*, Chapter 40.

CHAPTER XXXI

From Maximian, God the avenger of religion and of His people, turned His eyes to Galerius, the author of the accursed persecution, that in his punishment also He might manifest the power of His majesty. Galerius too was purposing to celebrate his twentieth anniversary.[1] And as under that pretext he had oppressed the provinces by new taxes payable in gold and silver, so now that he might recompense them by celebrating the promised festival, he used the like pretext for repeating his oppressions.

Who can relate in fit terms the methods used to harass mankind in levying the tax, and especially with regard to corn and the other fruits of the earth? The officers, or rather the executioners, of all the different magistrates seized on each individual and would never let go their hold. No man knew to whom he ought to make payment first. There was no dispensation given to those who had nothing, and they were required under pain of being variously tortured to pay instantly notwithstanding their inability. Many guards were set round, no breathing time was granted, nor at any season of the year the least respite from exactions. Different magistrates or the officers of different magistrates frequently contended for the right of levying the tax from the same persons. There would be no threshing-floor without a tax-gatherer, no vintage without a watch, and nothing left for the sustenance of the husbandman! That food should be snatched from the mouths of those who had earned it by toil was grievous. The hope, however, of being afterwards relieved might have made that grievance supportable, but it was necessary for every one who appeared at the anniversary festival to provide robes of various kinds and gold and silver besides. And one might have said, "How

56

shall I furnish myself with those things, O tyrant void of understanding, if you carry off the whole fruits of my ground and violently seize its expected produce?"

Thus, throughout the dominions of Galerius, men were despoiled of their goods and all was raked together into the imperial treasury that the emperor might be enabled to perform his vow of celebrating a festival which he was doomed never to celebrate.

NOTES

1. Galerius was elevated to the rank of Cæsar in AD 293 which meant that he would celebrate his Vicennalia (or the 20th year of his reign) beginning in AD 312. It should be noted that Lactantius points out in this work that three members of the first Tetrarchy either celebrated or planned to celebrate their Vicennalia—Diocletian, Maximian and Galerius. They would be the first emperors since Antoninus Pius (who ruled 22 years from AD 138–161) to celebrate this milestone. It should also be noted that Constantine would reach a Tricennalia, or 30th anniversary of his rule, in AD 336.

CHAPTER XXXII

Maximin Daia was incensed at the nomination of Licinius to the dignity of emperor, and he would no longer be called Cæsar or allow himself to be ranked as third in authority.[1] Galerius, by repeated messages, besought Daia to yield and to acquiesce in his arrangement, to give place to age and to reverence the grey hairs of Licinius. But Daia became more and more insolent. He urged that as it was he who first assumed the purple, so by possession he had right to priority in rank. And he set at nought the entreaties and the injunctions of Galerius. That brute animal was stung to the quick and bellowed when the mean creature whom he had made Cæsar, in expectation of his thorough obsequiousness, forgot the great favor conferred on him and impiously withstood the requests and will of his benefactor.

Galerius at length, overcome by the obstinacy of Daia, abolished the subordinate title of Cæsar, gave to himself and Licinius that of the Augusti and to Daia and Constantine that of sons of the Augusti. Daia, some time after, in a letter to Galerius, took occasion to observe that at the last general muster he had been saluted by his army under the title of Augustus. Galerius, vexed and grieved at this, commanded that all the four should have the appellation of emperor.[2]

NOTES

1. Galerius had raised Licinius to the supreme authority as Augustus in Chapter XXIX as the successor to Severus.
2. Eusebius largely concurs and supports Lactantius's account of events surrounding Maximin Daia's complaints over rank. See *Ecclesiastical History*, Book VIII, Chapter 13.

CHAPTER XXXIII

And now, when Galerius was in the eighteenth year of his reign, God struck him with an incurable plague.[1] A malignant ulcer formed itself low down in his secret parts and spread by degrees. The physicians attempted to eradicate it and healed up the place affected. But the sore, after having been skinned over, broke out again. A vein burst and the blood flowed in such quantity as to endanger his life. The blood, however, was stopped, although with difficulty. The physicians had to undertake their operations anew, and at length they cicatrized the wound.[2] In consequence of some slight motion of his body, Galerius received a hurt and the blood streamed more abundantly than before. He grew emaciated, pallid, and feeble, and the bleeding then stanched. The ulcer began to be insensible to the remedies applied, and a gangrene seized all the neighboring parts. It diffused itself the wider as more corrupted flesh was cut away, and everything employed as the means of cure served but to aggravate the disease.

"The masters of the healing arts withdrew, Chiron, sprung from Phillyra, and Amythaon's son, Melampus."[3]

Then famous physicians were brought in from all quarters, but no human means had any success. Apollo and Æsculapius were besought importunately for remedies. Apollo did prescribe and the distemper augmented. Already approaching to its deadly crisis, it had occupied the lower regions of his body. His bowels came out, and his whole seat putrefied. The luckless physicians, although without hope of overcoming the malady, ceased not to apply fomentations and administer medicines. The humors having been repelled, the distemper attacked his intestines, and worms were generated in his body. The stench was so foul as to pervade not only the palace, but even the whole city—and no wonder for by that time the passages from his bladder and bowels, having been devoured by the worms, became indiscriminate, and his body, with intolerable anguish, was dissolved into one mass of corruption.

"He lifted up his agonized bellows, like a bull that roars death-wounded as he flees from the altar,"[4]

They applied warm flesh of animals to the chief seat of the disease, that the warmth might draw out those minute worms. And accordingly when the dressings were removed, there issued forth an innumerable swarm. Nevertheless the prolific disease had hatched swarms much more abundant to prey upon and consume his intestines. Already, through a complication of distempers, the different parts of his body had lost their natural form: the superior part was dry, meagre, and haggard, and his ghastly-looking skin had settled itself deep amongst his bones, while the inferior, distended like bladders, remained no appearance of feet.

These things happened in the course of a complete year, and at length overcome by calamities, he was obliged to acknowledge God, and he cried aloud in the intervals of raging pain, that he would re-edify the Church which he had demolished and make atonement for his misdeeds.[5] And when he was near his end, he published an edict of the tenor following—

NOTES

1. Compare Eusebius's more abbreviated account of the horrific demise of Galerius in *Ecclesiastical History,* Book VIII, Chapter 16. See also for comparison, the deaths of Antiochus IV as recorded in 2 Maccabees 9 and Herod Agrippa in Acts 12:23.
2. To cicatrize a wound is to induce healing by encouraging the formation of scar tissue. Writing in the 1st century AD, Celsus details the use of this method to cure ulcers which appear in the genital area. See *On Medicine*, Book VII, Chapter 22.
3. Here Lactantius cites Virgil's *Georgics*, a poetic work focusing on agricultural themes. This particular quote is lifted from a section in which Virgil describes the devastation wrought by a plague among the animals and the inability of even the greatest human physicians to cope with it. See *Georgics,* Book III: 549–550.
4. Lactantius returns to Virgil's *Æneid* Book II:222–223 for this quote, which appears in the famous scene where Laocöon and his sons are slain by a sea serpent for their impiety toward the sacred wooden horse of Pallas Athena.
5. The claim that Galerius turned to the Christian God whom he had despised is supported by Eusebius in both the *Ecclesiastical History* (Book VIII, Chapter 17) and *Life of the Blessed Emperor Constantine* (Book I, Chapter 57).

CHAPTER XXXIV[1]

"Amongst our other regulations for the permanent advantage of the commonweal, we have hitherto studied to reduce all things to a conformity with the ancient laws and public discipline of the Romans. It has been our aim in an especial manner that the Christians also, who had abandoned the religion of their forefathers, should return to right opinions. For such willfulness and folly had, we know not how, taken possession of them, that instead of observing those ancient institutions which possibly their own forefathers had established, they, through caprice, made laws to themselves and drew together into different societies many men of widely different persuasions.

"After the publication of our edict, ordaining the Christians to betake themselves to the observance of the ancient institutions, many of them were subdued through the fear of danger and moreover many of them were exposed to jeopardy. Nevertheless, because great numbers still persist in their opinions and because we have perceived that at present they neither pay reverence and due adoration to the gods, nor yet worship their own God, therefore we from our wonted clemency in bestowing pardon on all, have judged it fit to extend our indulgence to those men and to permit them again to be Christians and to establish the places of their religious assemblies, so long as they do not offend against good order. By another mandate we purpose to signify unto magistrates what they need to observe.[2]

"Wherefore it will be the duty of the Christians, in consequence of this our toleration, to pray to their God for our welfare and for that of the public and for their own, that the commonweal may continue safe in every quarter and that they themselves may live securely in their habitations."[3]

NOTES

1. Here Lactantius provides in full Galerius's formal edict repealing the Great Persecution, written originally in Latin. Compare with Eusebius's Greek text as translated in *Ecclesiastical History*, Book VIII, Chapter 17.

2. It seems that Galerius died before he was able to promulgate this second edict.

3. Here Galerius reveals the rationale behind the persecution, namely that Christians had failed to observe the obligations of Roman citizens and had made a law unto themselves. Barnes considers this edict "revolutionary" in that it was the first attempt to reconcile Christian practice with good Roman citizenship by encouraging Christians to offer prayers to their God for the benefit of the Roman state. See *The Making of a Christian Empire*, pages 55–56.

CHAPTER XXXV

This edict was promulgated at Nicomedia on the day preceding the kalends of May, in the eighth consulship of Galerius and the second of Maximin Daia.[1] Then the prison-gates having been thrown open, you, my best beloved Donatus,[2] together with the other confessors for the faith, were set at liberty from a jail which had been your residence for six years.

Galerius, however, did not by publication of this edict obtain the divine forgiveness. In a few days after, he was consumed by the horrible disease that had brought on an universal putrefaction. Dying, he recommended his wife and son[3] to Licinius, and delivered them over into his hands. This event was known at Nicomedia before the end of the month. His vicennial anniversary was to have been celebrated on the ensuing kalends of March.[4]

NOTES

1. That is, April 30, AD 311.

2. Here Lactantius refers to the same Donatus to whom the work is

dedicated, and who is mentioned in Chapters I and XVI.
3.   Galerius's wife was Valeria, the daughter of Diocletian, as
      previously mentioned in Chapter XV of the present work as having
      possibly been a secret Christian. His son, Candidianus, was born
      of a concubine and later adopted by Valeria. He was previously
      mentioned in Chapter XX. Both would subsequently come into
      difficulties under Maximin Daia (see Chapter XXXIX), and to bad
      ends under Licinius (see Chapters L and LI).
4.   March 1, AD 312. Thus, Galerius perished before he was able to
      begin the celebration of his Vicennalia.

CHAPTER XXXVI

Daia, on receiving this news, hastened with relays of horses
from the East to seize the dominions of Galerius and, while
Licinius lingered in Europe, to arrogate to himself all the
country as far as the narrow seas of Chalcedon.[1] On entering
into Bithynia, with the view of acquiring immediate
popularity, he abolished Galerius's tax to the great joy of
all. Dissension arose between the two emperors and almost
an open war. They stood on the opposite shores with their
armies. Peace, however, and amity were established under
certain conditions. Licinius and Daia met on the narrow
straits, concluded a treaty, and in token of friendship joined
hands.

Then Daia, believing all things to be in security, returned
(to Nicomedia) and was in his new dominions what he had
been in Syria and Egypt. First of all, he took away the
toleration and general protection granted by Galerius to the
Christians and, for this end, he secretly procured addresses
from different cities, requesting that no Christian church
might be built within their walls. And thus he meant to make
that which was his own choice appear as if extorted from
him by importunity. In compliance with those addresses, he
introduced a new mode of government in things respecting
religion, and for each city he created a high priest chosen

from among the persons of most distinction. The office of those men was to make daily sacrifices to all their gods and, with the aid of the former priests, to prevent the Christians from erecting churches or from worshipping God either publicly or in private, and he authorized them to compel the Christians to sacrifice to idols and, on their refusal, to bring them before the civil magistrate. And, as if this had not been enough, in every province he established a superintendent priest, one of chief eminence in the state, and he commanded that all those priests newly instituted should appear in white habits, that being the most honorable distinction of dress. And as to the Christians, he purposed to follow the course that he had followed in the East and affecting the show of clemency, he forbade the slaying of God's servants, but he gave command that they should be mutilated. So the confessors for the faith had their ears and nostrils slit, their hands and feet lopped off, and their eyes dug out of the sockets.[2]

NOTES

1. Chalcedon is on the sea of Marmara, roughly opposite Byzantium on the southern end of the Bosporus. Lactantius indicates that Licinius took possession of Galerius's former territories in Europe, while Maximin seized Asia Minor.

2. Eusebius offers many additional details concerning this renewal of the persecution, saying that Maximin took the attacks on Christians to new extremes. Among the actions taken was the posting of anti-Christian imperial rescripts on brazen pillars set up in various cities throughout Maximin's domains. He also offered anti-Christian polemical works such as the forged Acts of Pilate in public places and introduced them to students for memorization. Numerous bishops, clergy, and lay Christians also suffered exile and death, and Eusebius recounts that this persecution, "seemed far more cruel than the former." See *Ecclesiastical History,* Book IX, Chapters 2–7.

   For additional evidence on Maximin's renewal of the persecution, including a Latin inscription from the time in the city of Calbasa in Asia Minor, see Mitchell, "Maximinus and the

Christians in AD 312: A New Latin Inscription," in *The Journal of Roman Studies* (1988), Vol. 78, pages 105–124

CHAPTER XXXVII

While occupied in this plan, he received letters from Constantine which deterred him from proceeding in its execution,[1] so for a time he dissembled his purpose.[2] Nevertheless any Christian that fell within his power was privily thrown into the sea. Neither did he cease from his custom of sacrificing every day in the palace. It was also an invention of his to cause all animals used for food to be slaughtered, not by cooks, but by priests at the altars, so that nothing was ever served up unless foretasted, consecrated, and sprinkled with wine according to the rites of paganism. And whoever was invited to an entertainment must needs have returned from it impure and defiled.

In all things else he resembled his preceptor Galerius. For if anything chanced to have been left untouched by Diocles and Maximian, that did Daia greedily and shamelessly carry off. And now the granaries of each individual were shut, and all warehouses sealed up, and taxes not yet due were levied by anticipation. Here famine arose even though the fields were cultivated, and in other places, prices of all things enhanced beyond measure. Herds and flocks were driven from their pasture for the daily sacrifice.[3] By gorging his soldiers with the flesh of sacrifices, he so corrupted them that they disdained their wonted pittance in corn and wantonly threw it away. Meanwhile Daia recompensed his bodyguards, who were very numerous, with costly raiment and gold medals, made donatives in silver to the common soldiers and recruits, and bestowed every sort of largesse on the barbarians who served in his army. As to grants of the property of living persons which he made to his favorites whenever they chose to ask for what belonged to another, I know not whether the same thanks might not be due to him that are given to merciful robbers who spoil without murdering.

NOTES

1. Comparing this with Eusebius's *Ecclesiastical History*, Book IX, Chapter 9, the correspondence here mentioned by Lactantius would seem to be (or include) the so-called Edict of Milan. However, scholars are divided as to whether these letters refer to the Edict, or to some other correspondence which has not survived. Baynes offers a reconstruction of the timeline of events which allows for two separate correspondences. See "Two Notes on the Great Persecution," page 193–194.

2. Eusebius records a letter from Maximin Daia to Sabinus, his prætorian prefect, which appears to show Maximin acceding to the demands of Constantine and Licinius that the Christians be afforded toleration in his realms. See *Ecclesiastical History*, Book IX, Chapter 9. Lactantius, like Eusebius, maintains that Maximin was far from sincere in actually suppressing the persecution, saying that the decree of Maximin was not regarded as trustworthy by Christians because he had acted deceitfully in renewing the persecution after Galerius ended it prior to his death. Interestingly, this variability of Maximin's character may have a somewhat different explanation. It is recorded by Eusebius and echoed by Aurelius Victor that Maximin was overly fond of wine, and that his harsh measures were often enacted while his mind was besotted and later repented of when he was sober. See *Ecclesiastical History*, Book VIII, Chapter 14 and *De Cæsaribus*, Chapter 40.

3. Famine and inflation in Maximin's domains are confirmed by the account in Eusebius who also adds that Maximin was defeated by the Armenians on the eastern frontier. He further details a plague that raged throughout the east at that time, saying that this litany of disasters was, "the rewards of the boasting of Maximinus and of the measures of the cities against us." See *Ecclesiastical History*, Book IX, Chapter 8.

CHAPTER XXXVIII

But that which distinguished his character, and in which he transcended all former emperors, was his desire of debauching women.[1] What else can I call it but a blind and headstrong passion? Yet such epithets feebly express my indignation in reciting his enormities. The magnitude of the guilt overpowers my tongue and makes it unequal to its office. Eunuchs and panders made search everywhere, and no sooner was any comely face discovered than husbands and parents were obliged to withdraw. Matrons of quality and virgins were stripped of their robes and all their limbs were inspected lest any part should be unworthy of the bed of the emperor. Whenever a woman resisted, death by drowning was inflicted on her, as if under the reign of this adulterer chastity had been treason. Some men there were who, beholding the violation of wives whom for virtue and fidelity they affectionately loved, could not endure their anguish of mind and so killed themselves. While this monster ruled, it was singular deformity alone which could shield the honor of any female from his savage desires. At length he introduced a custom prohibiting marriage unless with the imperial permission, and he made this an instrument to serve the purposes of his lewdness. After having debauched freeborn maidens, he gave them for wives to his slaves.

His courtiers also imitated the example of the emperor and violated with impunity the beds of their dependants. For who was there to punish such offenses? As for the daughters of men of middle rank, any who were inclined took them by force. Ladies of quality who could not be taken by force, were petitioned for and obtained from the emperor by way of free gift. Nor could a father oppose this, for the imperial warrant having been once signed, he had no alternative but to die or to receive some barbarian as his son-in-law. For very few of the henchmen at the emperor's side were other than the people who, having been driven from their habitations by the Goths in the twentieth year of Diocletian, yielded themselves to Galerius and entered into his service.[2] It was ill for humankind that men who had fled from the bondage of barbarians should thus come to lord it over the Romans. Environed by such guards, Daia oppressed and insulted the Eastern Empire.

NOTES

1. Compare to Eusebius who says that Maximin committed adultery on a monumental scale and could not pass by any city without continually corrupting its women. See *Ecclesiastical History*, Book VIII, Chapter 14.

2. That is, in AD 304. This is possibly a reference to the Carpi whom Diocletian and Galerius are often given credit for defeating in AD 303–304, as well as during previous campaigns along the Danube. It is worth noting that Lactantius indicates in Chapter XVII of the present work that Diocletian inspected the fortifications along the Danube frontier in AD 304 on his way back from Rome. Based on the titles he assumed at the time of his promotion to Augustus in AD 305, it may be deduced that Galerius was victorious over the Carpi along the Danube between AD 301 and 304. Writing in the 6th century, Jordanes records that Diocletian and Galerius were victorious over the Carpi and made them tributaries of the Roman Empire. See *The Gothic History of Jordanes,* Chapter 16. It is very likely that Maximian Daia was with Galerius during these campaigns and not unreasonable to assume that many of his henchmen would have been Carpi. See Barnes, "Imperial Campaigns: AD 285–311," in *Phoenix*, Vol. 30, No. 2, page 191.

CHAPTER XXXIX

Now Daia, in gratifying his libidinous desires, made his own will the standard of right, and therefore he would not refrain from soliciting the widow of Galerius, the Empress Valeria to whom he had lately given the appellation of mother. After the death of her husband, she had repaired to Daia because she imagined that she might live with more security in his dominions than elsewhere, especially as he was a married man.[1] But the flagitious creature became instantly inflamed with a passion for her. Valeria was still clothed in black, the time of her mourning not being yet expired. He sent a message to her proposing marriage and offering, on her compliance, to put away his wife.[2]

She frankly returned an answer such as she alone could dare to do: first, that she would not treat of marriage while she was in mourning and while the ashes of Galerius, her husband and, by adoption, the father of Daia, were yet warm. Next, that he acted impiously in proposing to divorce a faithful wife to make room for another whom in her turn he would also cast off. And lastly, that it was indecent, unexampled, and unlawful for a woman of her title and dignity to engage a second time in wedlock.[3]

This bold answer having been reported to Daia, presently his desires changed into rage and furious resentment. He pronounced sentence of forfeiture against the princess, seized her goods, removed her attendants, tortured her eunuchs to death, and banished her and her mother Prisca. But he appointed no particular place for her residence while in banishment, and hence he insultingly expelled her from every abode that she took in the course of her wanderings. And to complete all, he condemned the ladies who enjoyed most of her friendship and confidence to die on a false accusation of adultery.

NOTES

1. The name of Maximin's wife has not been recorded. Lactantius mentions later that this woman would be put to death by Licinius who had her thrown into the Orontes River. See Chapter L.

2. Given the precarious political situation of Maximin at this point, it is likely that his enflamed passions had more to do with political maneuvering for an alliance with Diocletian's family than with any sort of physical attraction.
3. Recall that in Chapter 15 of the present work, Lactantius insinuates that Valeria may have been a secret Christian, though likely an apostate forced to sacrifice to the pagan divinities by her husband, Galerius. Thus, her answer here shows certain characteristics that would be more expected of a Christian than a traditional Roman.

CHAPTER XL

There was a certain matron of high rank who already had grandchildren by more than one son. Valeria loved this woman like a second mother, and Daia suspected that her advice had produced that refusal which Valeria gave to his matrimonial offers. And therefore he charged the president Eratineus[1] to have her put to death in a way that might injure her fame. To her, two others equally noble were added. One of them, who had a daughter who was a Vestal virgin at Rome, maintained an intercourse by stealth with the banished Valeria. The other, married to a senator, was intimately connected with the empress. Excellent beauty and virtue proved the cause of their death.

They were dragged to the tribunal, not of an upright judge, but of a robber. Neither indeed was there any accuser until a certain Jew, one charged with other offenses, was induced through hope of pardon to give false evidence against the innocent. The equitable and vigilant magistrate conducted him out of the city under a guard lest the populace should have stoned him. This tragedy was acted at Nicæa. The Jew was ordered to the torture until he should speak as he had been instructed, while the torturers by blows prevented the women from speaking in their own defense. The innocent were condemned to die. Then there arose wailing and lamentation, not only of the senator who attended on his well-deserving consort, but amongst the spectators also whom this scandalous and unheard of proceeding had brought together. And, to prevent the multitude from violently rescuing the condemned persons out of the hands of the executioners, military commanders followed with light infantry and archers. And thus under a guard of armed soldiers, they were led to punishment. Their domestics having been forced to flee, they would have remained without burial had not the compassion of friends interred them by stealth.[2]

Nor was the promise of pardon made good to the feigned adulterer, for he was fixed to a gibbet and then he disclosed the whole secret contrivance, and with his last breath he protested to all the beholders that the women died innocent.

NOTES

1. The name "Eratineus" may be an interpolation by Lord Hailes, the English translator. Other translations of the work simply deem the individual in question as "the governor of Bithynia." See Creed's commentary on *De Mortibus Persecutorum*, Chapter 40, Note 2 on page 116. See also, Barnes, "More Missing Names, AD 260–395," in *Phoenix,* Vol. 27, No. 2, page 143.

2. It is worth comparing and contrasting this execution account with the martyrdoms endured by Christians during the persecutions. Compare, for example, the anonymous Passion of Saint Saturninus wherein the saint's body was allowed to lie unburied after his death until two Christian women surreptitiously retrieved and buried it in secret. See *On the Passion and Translation of Saint Saturninus, Bishop of the City of Toulouse and Martyr* as translated by Andrew Eastbourne and available at tertullian.org. In his account, Lactantius hints that these women are not Christians, to the point of mentioning the relation of one of them to a Vestal virgin, so his purpose here may have been to demonstrate to an audience of educated pagans that not even lofty status or traditional devotion to the pagan divinities are proof against the cruel machinations of the tyrants.

CHAPTER XLI

But the empress, an exile in some desert region of Syria, secretly informed her father Diocletian of the calamity that had befallen her. He despatched messengers to Daia requesting that his daughter might be sent to him. He could not prevail. Again and again he entreated, yet she was not sent. At length he employed a relation of his, a military man high in power and authority, to implore Daia by the remembrance of past favors. This messenger, equally unsuccessful in his negotiation as the others, reported to Diocletian that his prayers were in vain.[1]

NOTES

1. In this passage, Lactantius emphasizes the impotence of Diocletian who has now fallen so far from power that he is not even able to rescue his own wife and daughter from the torments of the barbaric Maximin. Lactantius is our only source for these events.

CHAPTER XLII

At this time, by command of Constantine, the statues of Maximian Herculius were thrown down and his portraits removed. And, as the two old emperors were generally delineated in one piece, the portraits of both were removed at the same time.[1] Thus Diocletian lived to see a disgrace which no former emperor had ever seen, and under the double load of vexation of spirit and bodily maladies, he resolved to die. Tossing to and fro with his soul agitated by grief, he could neither eat nor take rest. He sighed, groaned, and wept often, and incessantly threw himself into various postures, now on his couch, and now on the ground.

So he, who for twenty years was the most prosperous

of emperors, having been cast down into the obscurity of a private station,[2] treated in the most contumelious manner, and compelled to abhor life, became incapable of receiving nourishment and, worn out with anguish of mind, expired.[3]

NOTES

1. Lactantius shifts his focus now back to the West where Constantine instituted a *damnatio memoriæ* against the treacherous Maximian after his death. It does not appear that a formal decree of *damnatio memoriæ* was ever instituted against Diocletian. Indeed, Eutropius claims that he was "enrolled among the gods" upon his death. See *Breviarium*, Book IX, Chapter 28. That said, his memory was certainly condemned informally among the Christians whom he had persecuted. In that vein, Lactantius points out that Diocletian lived to see the destruction of his own monuments in tandem with those of Maximian. Thus, his death was accompanied not by extreme physical torment like that of Galerius, but by public humiliation and despondency.

2. It is worth noting that Eutropius considered Diocletian's voluntary resignation to private life to be an honorable act, perhaps reflecting the best ideals of the Roman Republic when men such as Lucius Quinticus Cincinnatus and Marcus Furius Camillus laid down the dictatorial power willingly. See *Breviarium*, Book IX, Chapter 28.

3. Other sources claim that Diocletian took his own life. Aurelius Victor holds that Diocletian was summoned by Constantine and Licinius to join them in celebrating a wedding (presumably that of Licinius to Constantine's half-sister Constantia in Milan in AD 313). When Diocletian balked, citing his ill health, rumors began to spread that he had favored Maxentius and Maximian. Fearing that he would be assassinated, Diocletian opted for poison. See *De Cæsaribus*, Chapter 39.

   The year of Diocletian's death has been the subject of scholarly debate. At first glance, it would appear from Lactantius that his death pre-dated Constantine's war with Maxentius, but it must be recalled that our present work does not follow a strict chronological order. For a fuller examination of Diocletian's death date, see Barnes, "Maxentius and Diocletian," in *Classical Philology*, Vol. 105, No. 3, pages 318–322.

   Though Lactantius provided Virgilian quotations to signal the death of Maximian (Chapter XXX) and Galerius (Chapter XXXIII), it is interesting that he does not do so for Diocletian.

CHAPTER XLIII

Of the adversaries of God there still remained one whose overthrow and end I am now to relate.

Daia had entertained jealousy and ill-will against Licinius from the time that the preference was given to him by Galerius, and those sentiments still subsisted notwithstanding the treaty of peace lately concluded between them.[1] When Daia heard that the sister of Constantine was betrothed to Licinius, he apprehended that the two emperors by contracting this affinity meant to league against him. So he privily sent ambassadors to Rome desiring a friendly alliance with Maxentius. He also wrote to him in terms of cordiality. The ambassadors were received courteously, friendship established, and in token of it, the effigies of Maxentius and Daia were placed together in public view.[2] Maxentius willingly embraced this as if it had been an aid from heaven, for he had already declared war against Constantine, as if to revenge the death of his father Maximian. From this appearance of filial piety a suspicion arose that the detestable old man had but feigned a quarrel with his son that he might have an opportunity to destroy his rivals in power, and so make way for himself and his son to possess the whole empire.[3] This conjecture, however, had no foundation, for his true purpose was to have destroyed his son and the others and then to have reinstated himself and Diocletian in sovereign authority.

NOTES

1. Recall the beginning of Chapter XXXII of the present work.
2. This treaty is also mentioned briefly by Eusebius in his *Ecclesiastical History,* Book VIII, Chapter 14.
3. The theory that Maximian only feigned his falling-out with

Maxentius in order to disrupt the rule of Constantine in Gaul is mentioned by Eutropius. See *Breviarium,* Book X, Chapter 3.

CHAPTER XLIV

And now a civil war broke out between Constantine and Maxentius.[1] Although Maxentius kept himself within Rome, because the soothsayers had foretold that if he went out of it he should perish, yet he conducted the military operations by able generals.[2] In forces he exceeded his adversary, for he had not only his father's army which deserted from Severus, but also his own which he had lately drawn together out of Mauritania and Italy.[3] They fought and the troops of Maxentius prevailed.[4] At length, Constantine with steady courage and a mind prepared for every event, led his whole forces to the neighborhood of Rome and encamped them opposite to the Milvian bridge. The anniversary of the reign of Maxentius approached—that is, the sixth of the kalends of November—and the fifth year of his reign was drawing to an end.[5]

Constantine was directed in a dream to cause the heavenly sign to be delineated on the shields of his soldiers and so to proceed to battle.[6] He did as he had been commanded, and he marked on their shields the letter X, with a perpendicular line drawn through it and turned round thus at the top, being the cipher of Christ. Having this sign (☧), his troops stood to arms.[7] The enemies advanced but without their emperor, and they crossed the bridge.[8] The armies met and fought with the utmost exertions of valor,

"neither this side or that marked by flight."[9]

In the meantime a sedition arose at Rome and Maxentius was reviled as one who had abandoned all concern for the safety of the commonweal. And suddenly, while he exhibited the Circensian games on the anniversary of his reign, the people cried with one voice, "Constantine cannot be overcome!" Dismayed at this, Maxentius burst from the assembly, and having called some senators together, ordered the Sibylline books to be searched. In them it was found that:

> "On the same day the enemy of the Romans should perish."[10]

Led by this response to the hopes of victory, he went to the field. The bridge in his rear was broken down. At sight of that the battle grew hotter. The hand of the Lord prevailed, and the forces of Maxentius were routed. He fled towards the broken bridge, but the multitude pressing on him, he was driven headlong into the Tiber.[11]

This destructive war being ended, Constantine was acknowledged as emperor with great rejoicings by the senate and people of Rome.[12] And now he came to know the perfidy of Daia, for he found the letters written to Maxentius and saw the statues and portraits of the two associates which had been set up together. The senate, in reward of the valor of Constantine, decreed to him the title of Maximus (the Greatest), a title which Daia had always arrogated to himself.[13]

Daia, when he heard that Constantine was victorious and Rome freed, expressed as much sorrow as if he himself had been vanquished. But afterwards, when he heard of the decree of the senate, he grew outrageous, avowed enmity towards Constantine, and made his title of "the Greatest" a theme of abuse and raillery.

NOTES

1. The conflict between Constantine and Maxentius commenced in

early AD 312. How the war initially developed has been discussed in some detail in numerous works both ancient and modern. Eusebius claims that Constantine could no longer endure the tyrannous oppression of Maxentius, saying, "that life was without enjoyment to him as long as he saw the imperial city thus afflicted." See *Life of the Blessed Emperor Constantine,* Book I, Chapter 26. In subsequent chapters of the same work, Eusebius catalogs the crimes of Maxentius, including the ravishing of women, the wholesale slaughter of Romans, and the practice of cruel and disgusting magical arts. This view seems supported by Eutropius who writes that Maxentius, "was spreading death among the nobility by every possible kind of cruelty." See *Breviarium*, Book X, Chapter 4. The anonymous panegyricist of AD 312 provides a few more details, claiming that Maxentius had used the wealth of Rome to hire henchmen whose purpose was to dispossess Roman citizens of their goods, saying, "he filled all of Italy with thugs hired for every sort of villainy." See Nixon, *In Praise of the Later Roman Emperors,* page 299. Finally, Aurelius Victor mentions Maxentius's "inhuman brutality" in his order that Carthage be laid waste after the defeat of a mutiny of the African provinces under the governor Alexander. See *De Cæsaribus,* Chapter 40. Even Zosimus, writing from the pagan perspective, calls Maxentius cruel and licentious, claiming that he had designs on Rætia, Dalmatia and Illyricum, provinces that were under the control of Constantine and Licinius. See *New History*, Book II:14.

2.   Compare this passage with Zosimus who agrees that Maxentius at first remained within Rome, but later came out to do battle. See *New History,* Book II:16.

3.   According to Zosimus, Maxentius's forces amounted to 170,000, including the army he had enticed to his side from Severus (see Chapter XXVI of the present volume), soldiers of his own from Italy, and additional forces drawn from Sicily and Africa. See *New History,* Book II:15. The African troops had likely been freed up by Maxentius's recent victory over the mutinous forces of Alexander at Carthage. See Aurelius Victor, *De Cæsaribus,* Chapter 40.

        Constantine's forces, by contrast, numbered about 98,000 including Roman troops from Britain along with Germans and Celts whom he had conquered and now served under him. See *New History,* Book II:15.

4.   Some details of Constantine's campaign in Italy prior to reaching Rome may be reconstructed from other sources. Eusebius says that Maxentius positioned his troops throughout Italy with the intention of ambushing Constantine's army as it advanced. Constantine,

however, defeated Maxentius's generals in three battles before approaching Rome. See *Life of the Blessed Emperor Constantine,* Book I, Chapter XXXVII. The anonymous panegyricist, writing soon after Constantine's ultimate victory in this war, gives the sites of three victories as the towns of Susa, Turin and Verona along with numerous additional details. See Nixon, *In Praise of the Later Roman Emperors,* pages 303–315. Anonymous Valesianus confirms that a victorious battle was waged by Constantine over the forces of Maxentius at Verona (Book I, Chapter 4).

Lactantius's comment here that Maxentius had prevailed seems to indicate that Constantine found himself checked upon his arrival at Rome. His forces were likely still inferior to those of Maxentius, and the Aurelian Walls of Rome were considered impregnable with sufficient troops to guard them.

5. That is, October 27, AD 312.

6. Compare this version of the famous vision of Constantine to the more detailed account of Eusebius who records that Constantine and his soldiers together witnessed a vision of a cross in the heavens. Eusebius adds that Constantine subsequently experienced a dream wherein he saw a vision of Christ who commanded him to use the standard of the chi-rho (☧) as a safeguard for the coming battle. This second part of Eusebius's account corresponds closely to that of Lactantius. See *Life of the Blessed Emperor Constantine,* Book I, Chapter 28–29.

It is also worth noting that this vision was not the first theophany experienced by Constantine. One of the anonymous panegyricists notes that in the early years of his reign, Constantine experienced a vision of a god he thought was Apollo granting him laurel wreaths as tokens of a long life and successful reign. See Nixon, *In Praise of the Later Roman Emperors,* pages 248–250.

7. This is, of course, the Christian chi-rho symbol, though some have argued that it represents a staurogram, that is, a ligature of tau and rho (☧) representing the crucified Jesus. Eusebius mentions that at this time, Constantine also caused to be created the standard of the Cross known as the Labarum. See *Life of the Blessed Emperor Constantine,* Book I, Chapter XXX–XXXI.

8. According to Zosimus, the bridge over the Tiber was a pontoon bridge of sorts, divided into two parts and held together with iron pins. This was purposely set up so that the pins could be withdrawn once the Constantinian army was upon the bridge. See *New History,* Book II:15. Aurelius Victor adds that Maxentius later found himself ensnared by the very traps he had set for Constantine. See *De Cæsaribus,* Chapter 40. Eusebius mentions that Maxentius had built

a strong bridge of boats and had "framed an engine of destruction, really against himself, but in the hope of ensnaring thereby him who was beloved by God. See *Life of the Blessed Emperor Constantine,* Book I, Chapter 38. It seems reasonable to surmise that Constantine had gotten wind of these traps and hence had his army stand its ground on the far side of the Tiber to await the attack of the superior forces of Maxentius.

9. Lactantius here quotes Virgil's *Æneid*, Book 10, line 757.

10. The present work is the primary source for these details of the sedition in Rome. Lactantius is echoed by Zosimus writing from the pagan perspective some 200 years later who adds that Maxentius applied this tragically imprecise Sibylline warning to Constantine as he viewed himself as the defender of Rome. See *New History,* Book II:16.

11. Compare Lactantius's brief account of the battle to that of Eusebius in *Life of the Blessed Emperor Constantine*, Book I, Chapter 39 which is similar. Aurelius Victor claims that Maxentius perished after his horse slipped and he sank into the Tiber due to the weight of his armor. See *De Cæsaribus*, Chapter 40.

The most detailed account of the battle comes from Zosimus, who tells us that when Maxentius emerged from Rome, a great flock of owls descended upon the walls of Rome and perched there. Because of that, Constantine decided to hold his ground and the troops of Maxentius advanced toward him to do battle. But no sooner were Maxentius's forces in position than the cavalry of Constantine attacked, throwing Maxentius's line into disorder. Constantine's infantry then advanced, and a furious fight ensued with great numbers slain on each side. Zosimus maintains that the morale of Maxentius's soldiers was suspect as few of them wished to risk their lives to defend a tyrant. The cavalry of Maxentius broke and fled toward the bridge over the Tiber where their weight caused the bridge to collapse, plunging Maxentius and many of his men to their deaths. See *New History,* Book II:16.

12. The anonymous panegyricist of AD 312 provides a gruesome description of what happened in Rome following Constantine's victory. He says that the body of Maxentius was recovered from the Tiber and hacked to pieces. His head was placed on a spear and paraded around the city to be the subject of jests and disfigurement. See Nixon, *In Praise of the Later Roman Emperors*, page 322.

13. According to Eusebius, Constantine caused Rome to be decorated with monumental inscriptions celebrating his victory. He further ordered that a cross be placed beneath the hand of a statue representing himself in a busy part of Rome bearing an inscription

in Latin saying: "By virtue of this salutary sign, which is the true symbol of valor, I have preserved and liberated your city from the yoke of tyranny. I have also set at liberty the Roman senate and people, and restored them to their ancient greatness and splendor." See *Life of the Blessed Emperor Constantine*, Book I, Chapter 40.

The panegyricist of AD 312 provides additional embellishment for Constantine's triumphal progress through Rome, including mention of his visit to the palace and his speech before the Roman senate wherein he restored the senators to their former authority. See Nixon, *In Praise of the Later Roman Emperors,* page 322–325.

CHAPTER XLV

Constantine having settled all things at Rome, went to Milan about the beginning of winter.[1] Thither also Licinius came to receive his wife, Constantia.[2] When Daia understood that they were busied in solemnizing the nuptials, he moved out of Syria in the depth of a severe winter and by forced marches he came into Bithynia with an army much impaired, for he lost all his beasts of burden of whatever kind in consequence of excessive rains and snow, muddy roadways, cold and fatigue. Their carcasses, scattered about the roads, seemed an emblem of the calamities of the impending war, and the presage of a like destruction that awaited the soldiers.[3]

Daia did not halt in his own territories, but immediately crossed the Thracian Bosphorus, and in a hostile manner approached the gates of Byzantium. There was a garrison in the city, established by Licinius to check any invasion that Daia might make. At first Daia attempted to entice the soldiers by the promise of donatives, and then to intimidate them by assault and storm. Yet neither promises nor force availed aught. After eleven days had elapsed, within which time Licinius might have learned the state of the garrison, the soldiers surrendered, not through treachery but because they were too weak to make a longer resistance. Then Daia moved on to Heraclea (otherwise called Perinthus), and by delays of the like nature before that place lost some days. And now Licinius by expeditious marches had reached Adrianople, but with forces not numerous. Then Daia, having taken Perinthus by capitulation and remained there for a short space, moved forwards eighteen miles to the first station. Here his progress was stopped, for Licinius had already occupied the second station, at the distance also of eighteen miles. Licinius, having assembled what forces he could from the neighboring quarters, advanced towards Daia rather indeed to retard his operations than with any purpose of fighting or hope of victory, for Daia had an army of seventy thousand men, while he himself had scarcely thirty thousand. Licinius's soldiers were dispersed in various regions, and there was not time, on that sudden emergency, to collect all of them together.[4]

NOTES

1. The assumption here is that Constantine remained in Rome through the end of the year, arriving in Milan sometime in early AD 313.
2. By this marriage, Constantine and Licinius cemented their alliance. See previous mention of the betrothal of Licinius and Constantia in Chapter XLIII of the present volume.
3. Eusebius mentions that Maximin was weakened by a war with the previously allied Armenians in which his forces were defeated. The reason for the conflict, according to Eusebius, was that Maximin had attempted to force the largely Christian Armenians to sacrifice to pagan divinities. See *Ecclesiastical History*, Book IX, Chapter 8.
4. Lactantius here and in the following two chapters provides the most detailed information extant on the failed campaign of Maximin to take control of Licinius's European territories and his subsequent death. For a detailed look at the war between Licinius and Maximin, see Christensen, *C. Galerius Valerius Maximinus: Studies in the Politics and Religion of the Roman Empire, AD 305–313*, pages 294–307.

CHAPTER XLVI

The armies thus approaching each other, seemed on the eve of a battle. Then Daia made this vow to Jupiter, that if he obtained victory he would extinguish and utterly efface the name of the Christians. And on the following night an angel of the Lord seemed to stand before Licinius while he was asleep, admonishing him to arise immediately and with his whole army to put up a prayer to the Supreme God, and assuring him that by so doing he should obtain victory. Licinius dreamed that after hearing this, he arose, and that he who had warned him still stood by and directed how he should pray and in what words. Awaking from sleep, he sent for one of his secretaries and dictated these words exactly as he had heard them:

> "Supreme God, we beseech Thee. Holy God, we beseech Thee. Unto Thee we commend all justice. Unto Thee we commend our safety. Unto Thee we commend our empire. By Thee we live, by Thee we are victorious and happy. Supreme Holy God, hear our prayers. To Thee we stretch forth our arms. Hear, Holy Supreme God."[1]

Many copies were made of these words and distributed amongst the principal commanders, who were to teach them to the soldiers under their charge. At this all men took fresh courage, in the confidence that victory had been announced to them from heaven. Licinius resolved to give battle on the kalends of May, for precisely eight years before Daia had received the dignity of Cæsar,[2] and Licinius chose that day in hopes that Daia might be vanquished on the anniversary of his reign, as Maxentius had been on his.

Daia, however, purposed to give battle earlier, to fight

on the day before those kalends,[3] and to triumph on the anniversary of his reign. Accounts came that Daia was in motion, so the soldiers of Licinius armed themselves and advanced. A barren and open plain, called Campus Serenus, lay between the two armies. They were now in sight of one another. The soldiers of Licinius placed their shields on the ground, took off their helmets and, following the example of their leaders, stretched forth their hands towards heaven. Then the emperor uttered the prayer and they all repeated it after him. The host, doomed to speedy destruction, heard the murmur of the prayers of their adversaries. And now, the ceremony having been thrice performed, the soldiers of Licinius became full of courage, buckled on their helmets again, and resumed their shields.

The two emperors advanced to a conference, but Daia could not be brought to peace for he held Licinius in contempt and imagined that the soldiers would presently abandon an emperor parsimonious in his donatives and enter into the service of one liberal even to profusion. And indeed it was on this notion that he began the war. He looked for the voluntary surrender of the armies of Licinius, and thus reinforced, he meant forthwith to have attacked Constantine.[4]

NOTES

1. Compare this account of Licinius's dream to that of Constantine in Chapter XLIV of the present work. It is also worth comparing the text of this prayer to that of Constantine as recorded by Eusebius in *Life of the Blessed Emperor Constantine*, Book IV, Chapter 20.
2. May 1, AD 313.
3. April 30, AD 303.
4. The strategy of Maximin in attempting to bribe the soldiers of his opponent to change sides echoes that of Maxentius in his struggles with Severus and Galerius. Maximin, however, miscalculated. Maxentius had held a strong defensive position at Rome and appealed to soldiers who had previously served or reverenced his

father, Maximian, who had reigned for nearly twenty years. In Maximin's case, his army had invaded enemy territory and, it is assumed, he was appealing to troops who had little reason to admire or trust him over Licinius. Pure greed, it seems, was not enough to motivate Licinius's soldiers to defect.

CHAPTER XLVII

So the two armies drew nigh, the trumpets gave the signal, the military ensigns advanced, and the troops of Licinius charged. But the enemies, panic-struck, could neither draw their swords nor yet throw their javelins. Daia went about and, alternately by entreaties and promises, attempted to seduce the soldiers of Licinius. But he was not hearkened to in any quarter, and they drove him back. Then were the troops of Daia slaughtered, none making resistance, and such numerous legions and forces so mighty were mowed down by an inferior enemy. No one called to mind his reputation, or former valor, or the honorable rewards which had been conferred on him. The Supreme God did so place their necks under the sword of their foes, that they seemed to have entered the field, not as combatants, but as men devoted to death.[1]

After great numbers had fallen, Daia perceived that everything went contrary to his hopes, and therefore he threw aside the purple and having put on the habit of a slave, hastened across the Thracian Bosphorus. One half of his army perished in battle and the rest either surrendered to the victor or fled. For now that the emperor himself had deserted, there seemed to be no shame in desertion. Before the expiration of the kalends of May, Daia arrived at Nicomedia, although distant one hundred and sixty miles from the field of battle. So in the space of one day and two nights he performed that journey. Having hurried away with his children and wife and a few officers of his court, he went towards Syria.[2] But having been joined by some troops from those quarters and having collected together a part of his fugitive forces, he halted in Cappadocia, and then he resumed the imperial garb.[3]

NOTES

1. Zosimus suggests that Licinius seemed in danger of defeat at first, but his forces rallied and proceeded to rout the host of Maximin. See *New History,* Book II:17.
2. Eusebius upbraids Maximin severely for fleeing in the guise of a private person and mentions that once he arrived back at his territories in the east, he slaughtered the pagan soothsayers who had forecasted his victory as imposters who endangered his safety. See *Ecclesiastical History*, Book IX, Chapter 10.
3. As pointed out by Christensen, Maximin was by no means beaten at this point and certainly had hopes of stopping Licinius in Asia Minor. See *C. Galerius Valerius Maximinus: Studies in the Politics and Religion of the Roman Empire, AD 305–313*, page 303.

CHAPTER XLVIII

Not many days after the victory, Licinius, having received part of the soldiers of Daia into his service and properly distributed them, transported his army into Bithynia and having made his entry into Nicomedia, he returned thanks to God through whose aid he had overcome. And on the ides of June,[1] while he and Constantine were consuls for the third time, he commanded the following edict for the restoration of the Church, directed to the president of the province, to be promulgated:[2]

"When we, Constantine and Licinius, emperors, had an interview at Milan and conferred together with respect to the good and security of the commonweal, it seemed to us that amongst those things that are profitable to mankind in general, the reverence paid to the Divinity merited our first and chief attention and that it was proper that the Christians and all others should have liberty to follow that mode of religion which to each of them appeared best, so that that God who is seated in heaven might be benign and propitious to us and to everyone under our government. And therefore we judged it a salutary measure and one highly consonant to right reason that no man should be denied leave of attaching himself to the rites of the Christians or to whatever other religion his mind directed him, that thus the supreme Divinity, to whose worship we freely devote ourselves, might continue to vouchsafe His favor and beneficence to us.

And accordingly we give you to know that without regard to any provisos in our former orders to you concerning the Christians, all who choose that religion are to be permitted, freely and absolutely, to remain in it and not to be disturbed in any way or molested. And we thought fit to communicate fully the things committed to your charge, that you might understand that the indulgence which we have granted in matters of religion to the Christians is ample and unconditional, and perceive at the same time that the open and free exercise of their respective religions is granted to all others as well as to the Christians. For it befits the well-ordered state and the tranquillity of our times that each individual be allowed, according to his own choice, to worship the Divinity. And we mean not to derogate aught from the honor due to any religion or its votaries.

Moreover, with respect to the Christians, we formerly gave certain orders concerning the places appropriated for their religious assemblies, but now we will that all persons who have purchased such places, either from our treasury or from any one else, do restore them to the Christians without money demanded or price claimed, and that this be performed peremptorily and unambiguously. And we will also that they who have obtained any right to such places by form of gift do forthwith restore them to the Christians: reserving always to such persons, who have either purchased for a price or gratuitously acquired them, to make application to the judge of the district if they look on themselves as entitled to any equivalent from our beneficence. All those places are, by your intervention, to be immediately restored to the Christians.

And because it appears that besides the places appropriated to religious worship, the Christians did possess other places which belonged not to individuals but to their society in general, that is, to their churches, we comprehend all such within the regulation aforesaid, and we will that you cause them all to be restored to the society or churches, and that without hesitation or controversy: provided always that the persons making restitution without a price paid shall be at liberty to seek indemnification from our bounty.

In furthering all of these things for the benefit of the Christians, you are to use your utmost diligence, to the end that our orders be speedily obeyed and our gracious purpose in securing the public tranquillity promoted. So shall that divine favor which in affairs of the mightiest importance we have already experienced, continue to give success to us and in our successes make the commonweal happy.[3] And that the tenor of this our gracious ordinance may be made known unto all, we will that you cause it by your authority to be published everywhere."

Licinius, having issued this ordinance, made a harangue in which he exhorted the Christians to rebuild their religious edifices. And thus, from the overthrow of the Church until its restoration, there was a space of ten years and about four months.[4]

NOTES

1. June 13, AD 313.
2. Here Lactantius records the momentous document traditionally known as the Edict of Milan. Modern scholars have endlessly debated both the appellation and the significance of this document. A lengthy summary of the arguments may be found in Anastos, "The Edict of Milan (313): A Defense of its Traditional Authorship and Designation," in *Revue de Études Byzantines*, Vol. 25, pages 13–41. Compare Lactantius's version with the decree of Licinius and Constantine recorded by Eusebius which he translated into Greek "from the Roman tongue." See *Ecclesiastical History*, Book X, Chapter 5.

   It is also worth comparing the tone and provisions of this document with the half-measures proposed by Galerius in Chapter XXXIV and Maximin in Chapter XXXVI of the present volume.
3. This sentiment—that those who serve and revere God will receive divine favors even in the greatest of affairs—is a perfect counterpoint to the main theme of the present work. Constantine will later echo this belief in a more nuanced way in a decree to the inhabitants of Palestine wherein he says: "To all who entertain just and wise sentiments respecting the character of the Supreme Being, it has long been most clearly evident…that they who faithfully observe His holy laws, and shrink from transgressions of His commandments, are rewarded with abundant blessings, and are endued with well-grounded hope as well as ample power for the accomplishment of their undertakings. On the other hand, they who have cherished impious sentiments have experienced results corresponding to their evil choice." See Eusebius, *Life of the Blessed Emperor Constantine*, Book II, Chapter XXIV. It is interesting to speculate whether (or how much) Lactantius influenced the emperor's thinking on these points.

   But lest we assume that Constantine's understanding of divine providence was merely a simplistic and easily falsifiable notion that God punishes the evil and rewards the good in the present life, later in the same decree we find the following passage: "Whoever have addressed themselves with integrity of purpose to any course of action, keeping the fear of God continually before their thoughts… such persons, though for a season they may have experienced painful trials, have borne their afflictions lightly, being supported by the belief of greater rewards in store for them."

4. Recall that the Great Persecution commenced in Nicomedia. See Chapter XII of the present volume. Therefore, the harangue of Licinius and the proclamation of the end of the persecution in Nicomedia must have had powerful symbolic value, particularly for the Christians in the Roman East.

CHAPTER XLIX

While Licinius pursued with his army, the fugitive tyrant retreated and again occupied the passes of mount Taurus. And there, by erecting parapets and towers, attempted to stop the march of Licinius. But the victorious troops, by an attack made on the right, broke through all obstacles, and Daia at length fled to Tarsus.

There, being hard pressed both by sea and land, he despaired of finding any place for refuge, and in the anguish and dismay of his mind, he sought death as the only remedy of those calamities that God had heaped on him. But first he gorged himself with food and large draughts of wine, as those are wont who believe that they eat and drink for the last time, and so he swallowed poison. However, the force of the poison, repelled by his full stomach, could not immediately operate but it produced a grievous disease resembling the pestilence, and his life was prolonged only that his sufferings might be more severe. And now the poison began to rage and to burn up everything within him so that he was driven to distraction with the intolerable pain. And during a fit of frenzy which lasted four days, he gathered handfuls of earth and greedily devoured it.

Having undergone various and excruciating torments, he dashed his forehead against the wall and his eyes started out of their sockets. And now, become blind, he imagined that he saw God with His servants arrayed in white robes sitting in judgment on him. He roared out as men on the rack are wont, and exclaimed that not he, but others, were guilty. In the end, as if he had been racked into confession, he acknowledged his own guilt and lamentably implored Christ to have mercy upon him. Then amidst groans, like those of one burnt alive, did he breathe out his guilty soul in the most horrible kind of death.[1]

NOTES

1. Lactantius is the only ancient source who calls Maximin's death the result of suicide. Eutropius, by contrast, indicates that his death was an accident. See *Breviarium* Book X, Chapter 4. Aurelius Victor says that he died a "simple death at Tarsus." See *De Cæsaribus*, Chapter 40. Zosimus says only that Maximin died in Tarsus while attempting to raise more troops to resist Licinius. See *New History*, Book II:17.

    Eusebius, however, provides two accounts of Maximin's death which are similar to that of Lactantius, but with a few key differences. In his *Ecclesiastical History*, Book IX, Chapter 10, Eusebius relates that Maximin contracted a grave illness while his soldiers were still active in the field fighting on his behalf. This sickness caused intolerable pains and the wasting of his body, along with intense fever. In the same vein as Lactantius, Eusebius reports that Maximin's eyes burst as a result of his illness and in his death throes, he confessed the Christian God and set forth an edict in favor of the Christians similar to that of Constantine and Licinius which Eusebius dutifully records.

    In *Life of the Blessed Emperor Constantine*, Book I, Chapters 58–59, Eusebius gives a slightly different account again, adding the detail that Maximin had put off the imperial garb and sought to conceal himself as a private person when he was struck down by God with a dread illness. It was only after considerable suffering that Maximin denounced the pagan pantheon and declared that "he now knew, by positive experience, that the God of the Christians was the only true God."

CHAPTER L

Thus did God subdue all those who persecuted His name, so that neither root nor branch of them remained. For Licinius, as soon as he was established in sovereign authority, commanded that Valeria should be put to death. Daia, although exasperated against her, never ventured to do this, not even after his discomfiture and flight and when he knew that his end approached.[1] Licinius commanded that Candidianus also should be put to death. He was the son of Galerius by a concubine, and Valeria, having no children, had adopted him. On the news of the death of Daia, she came in disguise to the court of Licinius, anxious to observe what might befall Candidianus. The youth, presenting himself at Nicomedia, had an outward show of honor paid to him and, while he suspected no harm, was killed.[2] Hearing of this catastrophe, Valeria immediately fled.

The Emperor Severus left a son, Severianus, who was now mature of years and who had accompanied Daia in his flight from the field of battle. Licinius caused him to be condemned and executed under the pretence that, on the death of Daia, he had intentions of assuming the imperial purple.[3] Long before this time, Candidianus and Severianus, apprehending evil from Licinius, had chosen to remain with Daia, while Valeria favored Licinius, though she was unwilling to bestow on him that which she had also denied to Daia—all rights accruing to her as the widow of Galerius.[4]

Licinius also put to death Maximus, the son of Daia—a boy eight years old, and a daughter of Daia who was seven years old and had been betrothed to Candidianus.[5] But before their death, their mother had been thrown into the Orontes, in which river she herself had frequently commanded chaste women to be drowned.[6] So, by the unerring and just judgment of God, all the impious received according to the deeds that they had done.[7]

NOTES

1. In this passage, Lactantius provides a hint that all was not right with Licinius, insinuating that he was, in some ways, worse and more ruthless than Maximin. For Valeria, the daughter of Diocletian and wife of Galerius, see the previous notes on Chapters XV, XXXV, and XXXIX.
2. Following the defeat and death of Maximin, Licinius adopted a policy of ruthlessly and systematically executing anyone who had even a tenuous claim to the empire within his dominions. Regarding Candidianus, see Note 3 of Chapter XXXV of the present volume. He would have been twelve or thirteen years old at the time of his slaying.
3. Lactantius provides the only extant information on Severianus, the son of Severus.
4. Here again, Lactantius hints at evil tendencies in Licinius.
5. Lactantius is our only source for the existence of these children.
6. Antioch is the likely site of the execution of Maximin's wife given that the Orontes River flowed through that city.
7. This sentence provides a fair summation of the entire purpose of *On the Deaths of the Persecutors*.

CHAPTER LI

Valeria too, who for fifteen months had wandered under a mean garb from province to province, was at length discovered in Thessalonica, apprehended together with her mother Prisca, and suffered capital punishment.[1] Both the ladies were conducted to execution—a fall from grandeur which moved the pity of the multitude of beholders that the strange sight had gathered together. They were beheaded and their bodies cast into the sea. Thus the chaste demeanor of Valeria and the high rank of her and her mother proved fatal to both of them.

NOTES

1.   Recall that Prisca was the wife of Diocletian. See Chapter XV, Note
     1 above for more on Valeria and Prisca. Lactantius is the only extant
     reliable source for the demise of these two women.

CHAPTER LII

I relate all those things on the authority of well-informed
persons, and I thought it proper to commit them to writing
exactly as they happened lest the memory of events so
important should perish and lest any future historian of the
persecutors should corrupt the truth, either by suppressing
their offenses against God or the judgment of God against
them. To His everlasting mercy ought we to render thanks,
that having at length looked on the earth, He deigned to
collect again and to restore His flock, partly laid waste
by ravenous wolves and partly scattered abroad, and to
extirpate those noxious wild beasts who had trod down its
pastures and destroyed its resting-places. Where now are
the surnames of the Jovii and the Herculii, once so glorious
and renowned amongst the nations—surnames insolently
assumed at first by Diocles and Maximian and afterwards
transferred to their successors? The Lord has blotted them
out and erased them from the earth.[1]

Let us therefore with exultation celebrate the triumphs
of God, and oftentimes with praises make mention of His
victory. Let us in our prayers, by night and by day, beseech
Him to confirm forever that peace which, after a warfare of
ten years, He has bestowed on His own.[2]

And do you above all others, my best beloved Donatus,[3]
who so well deserve to be heard, implore the Lord that it
would please Him propitiously and mercifully to continue
His pity towards His servants, to protect His people from
the machinations and assaults of the devil, and to guard the
now flourishing churches in perpetual felicity.

NOTES

1. Of the persecuting emperors, Maximian, Maxentius and Maximin all seem to have had their memories condemned. So in the case of those three, their names were quite literally blotted out in the traditional Roman sense.
2. By warfare, Lactantius is referring here to the Great Persecution which lasted just over ten years. See the end of Chapter XLVIII above.
3. At the end, Lactantius re-introduces Donatus to whom the work is dedicated. See Chapters I, XVI, and XXXV.

INDEX

95

INDEX

Also available in the *Christian Roman Empire* Series

For more information on this series, see our website at:
http://www.evolpub.com/CRE/CREseries.html

Printed in the USA
CPSIA information can be obtained
at www.ICGtesting.com
LVHW040946270823
756411LV00006B/208